we can all play CRICKET

Fred Apps
& Len Enoch

WHAT DO YOU NEED TO PLAY CRICKET?

A FRIEND OR SOME FRIENDS

A BALL

A BAT

A WICKET

A BIT OF SPACE

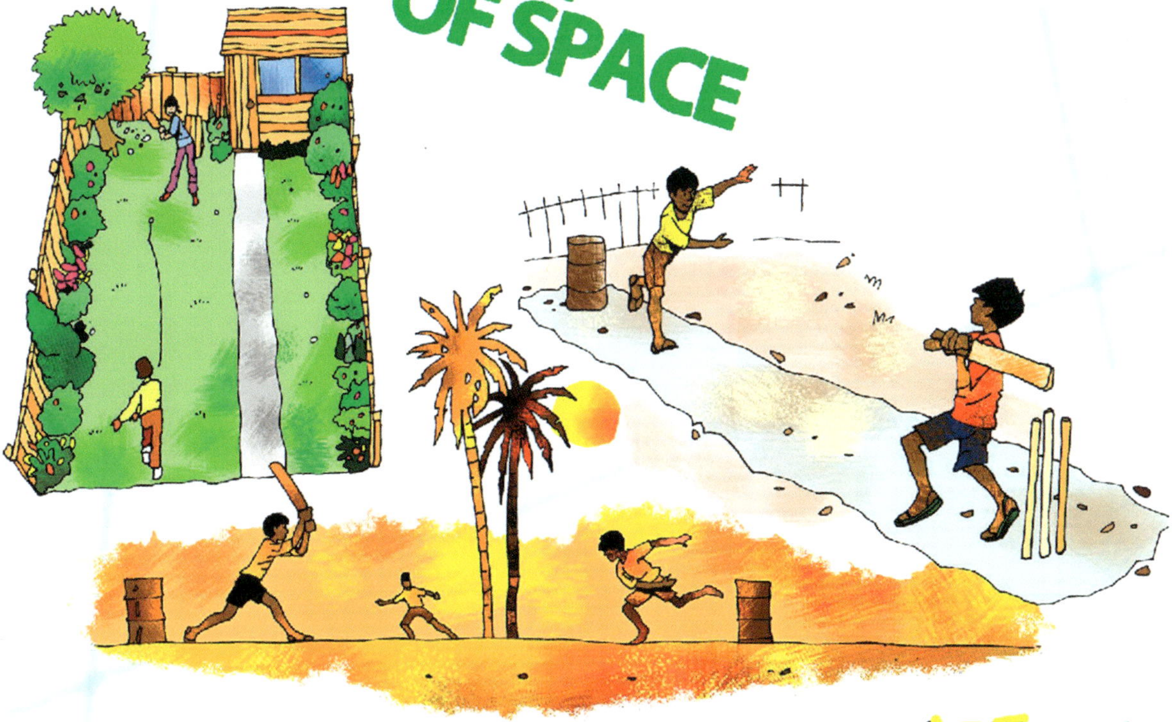

AND YOU'RE ON YOUR WAY!

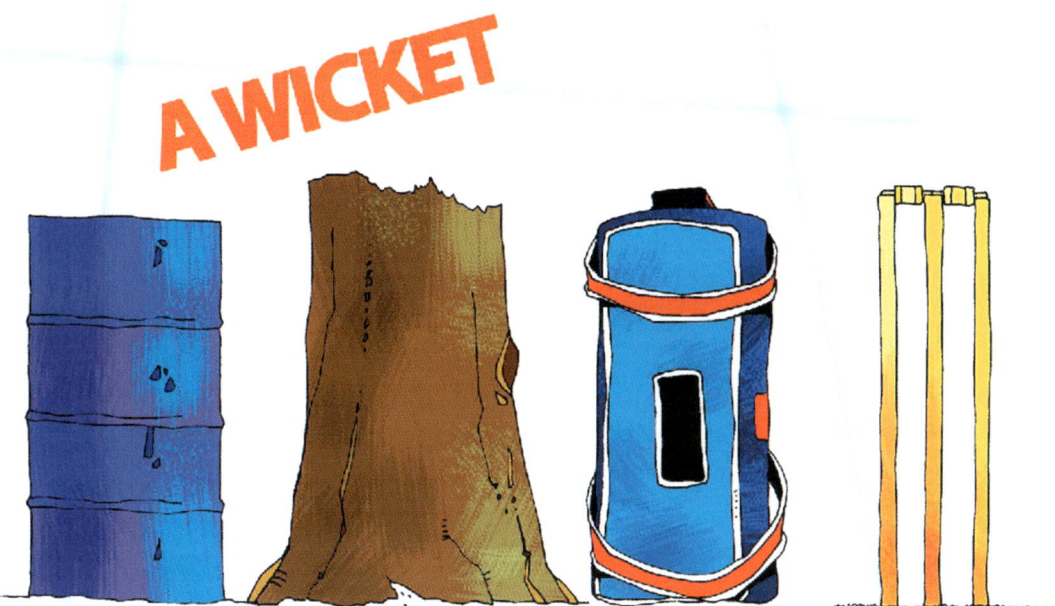

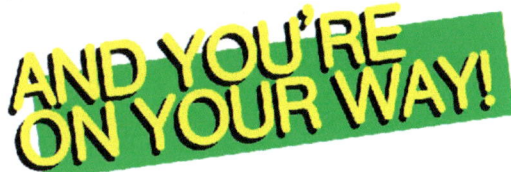

HOW CRICKET IS PLAYED

Two teams play each other. One team bats and the other team bowls and fields. Then they swap over.

The **BOWLER** bowls the ball towards the **BATTER six times**. This is called an **OVER**. The batter tries to hit the ball with the bat and run to the other end of the **PITCH**.

This is called a **RUN**.

If he or she misses and the ball hits the **STUMPS** the go (called the **INNINGS**) is finished and another batter takes over.

There are 9 other ways the batters innings can be finished - some of them are on this page - the rest you can find on p106. After the first over another bowler bowls six balls from the other end. Now everyone has to change positions and the **NON STRIKER** becomes the batter. If the batter hits the ball and it crosses the **BOUNDARY** 4 runs are scored. If it crosses the boundary in the air without bouncing first 6 runs are scored. When all the **batters** have finished their innings the **runs** are added up by the **SCORERS** to make the final score.

The batters from the other side now try to score more **runs**.

The runs are put on the **SCOREBOARD** and also written in the scorebook by the scorers.

UMPIRE 1

STUMPS - they have two bits of wood called **BAILS** balanced on top of them as a guide to show that they have been hit.

BOWLING CREASE

BATTER (non-striker)

6

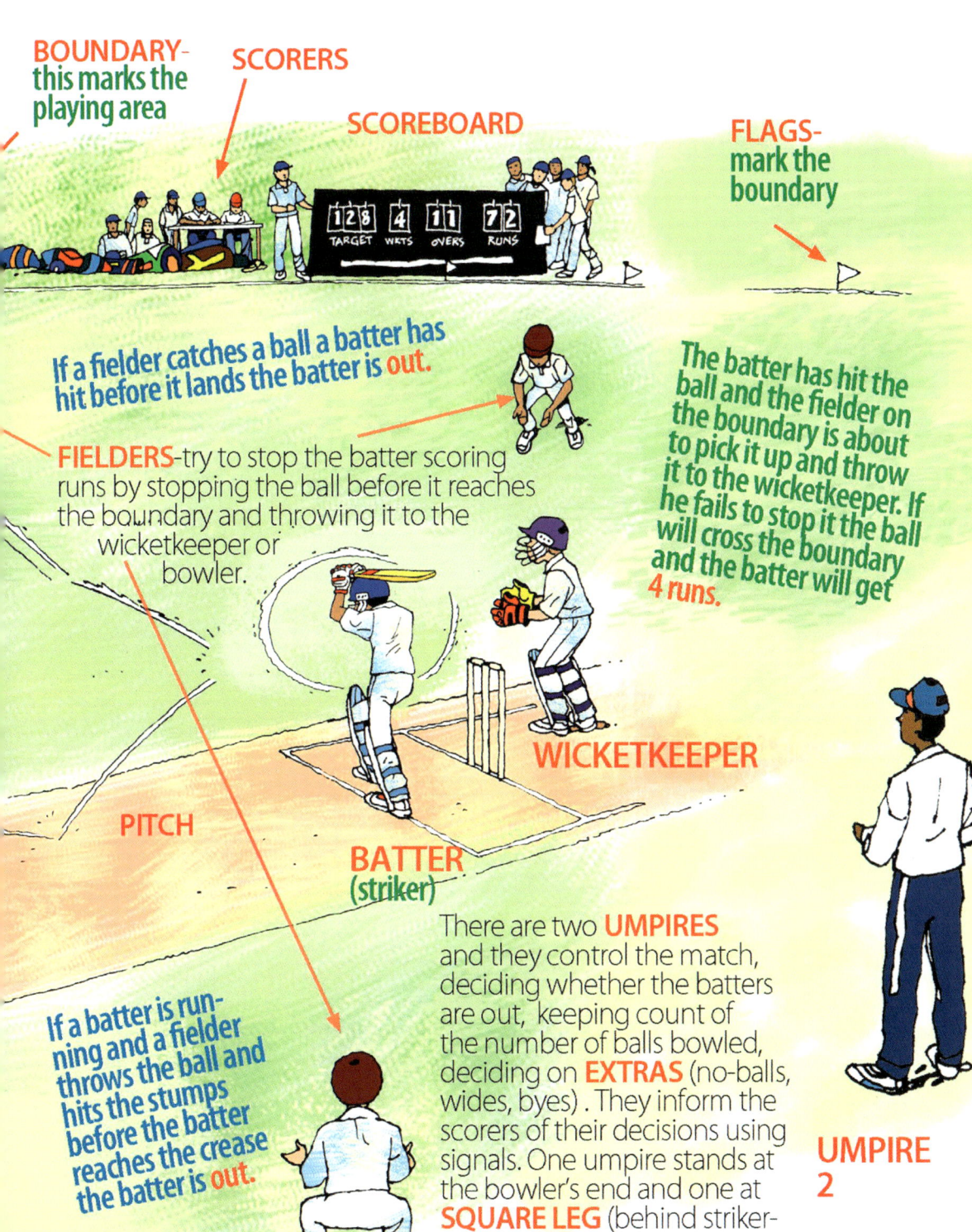

FIELDER

The **FIELDER'S** main job is to stop the ball after the BATTER has hit it and return it to the wicket keeper or bowler. The fielder also has to try to catch the ball before it bounces and run the batter out.

HSEL

As you go through the book a little symbol starts to appear - **HSEL**. This means **Head Still Eyes Level**. It's essential in every cricket skill! If your coach asks you a question about a skill you can always get on their right side by saying 'Head still eyes level'. But don't just parrot it - **think about it!**

BATTER

It's very simple – the **BATTER'S** job is to hit the ball with the bat and score runs. The more runs scored the more chance of winning the game

BOWLER

The **BOWLER** has two main jobs. The first is to get the **BATTER** out. The second is to stop the **BATTER** scoring **RUNS**

If the **BOWLER** hits the stumps with the ball the **BATTER** is out

This book is full of accurate pictures of every basic skill in cricket, with easy to follow steps of how the skills are done, plus lots of fun sheets. OK, you can't learn a sport from a book but having pictures and lots of information certainly helps! Study these skill sheets. Practice the stances in front of a mirror. If you like drawing try drawing out the poses for yourself (drawing something is a great way to get it in your head).

WICKET KEEPER

The **WICKET KEEPER'S** job is to stop the ball from the bowler if the batter misses and look for catches if the batter touches it with the bat. The wicket keeper will also look for **stumpings** if the batter moves down the pitch (see ways of getting out). The wicket keeper catches the ball and knocks the bails off to get **RUN OUTS**

There is more to every job as you will find out as you read through the book

CAPTAIN

Every side has a captain who decides who bowls and bats and where everyone stands in the field. It is a complicated job and more can be found out about it on p108

ABOUT FIELDING

You can quickly learn to be a *red hot* fielder—it's worth the hard work!

A captain doesn't send a fielder to stand just anywhere on the cricket field. There are named positions for them to stand in and they all have different jobs. To really understand the game of cricket you need to know those fielding positions! Have a look at the diagram — it shows you the names of some of the positions.

SOME FIELD PLACINGS

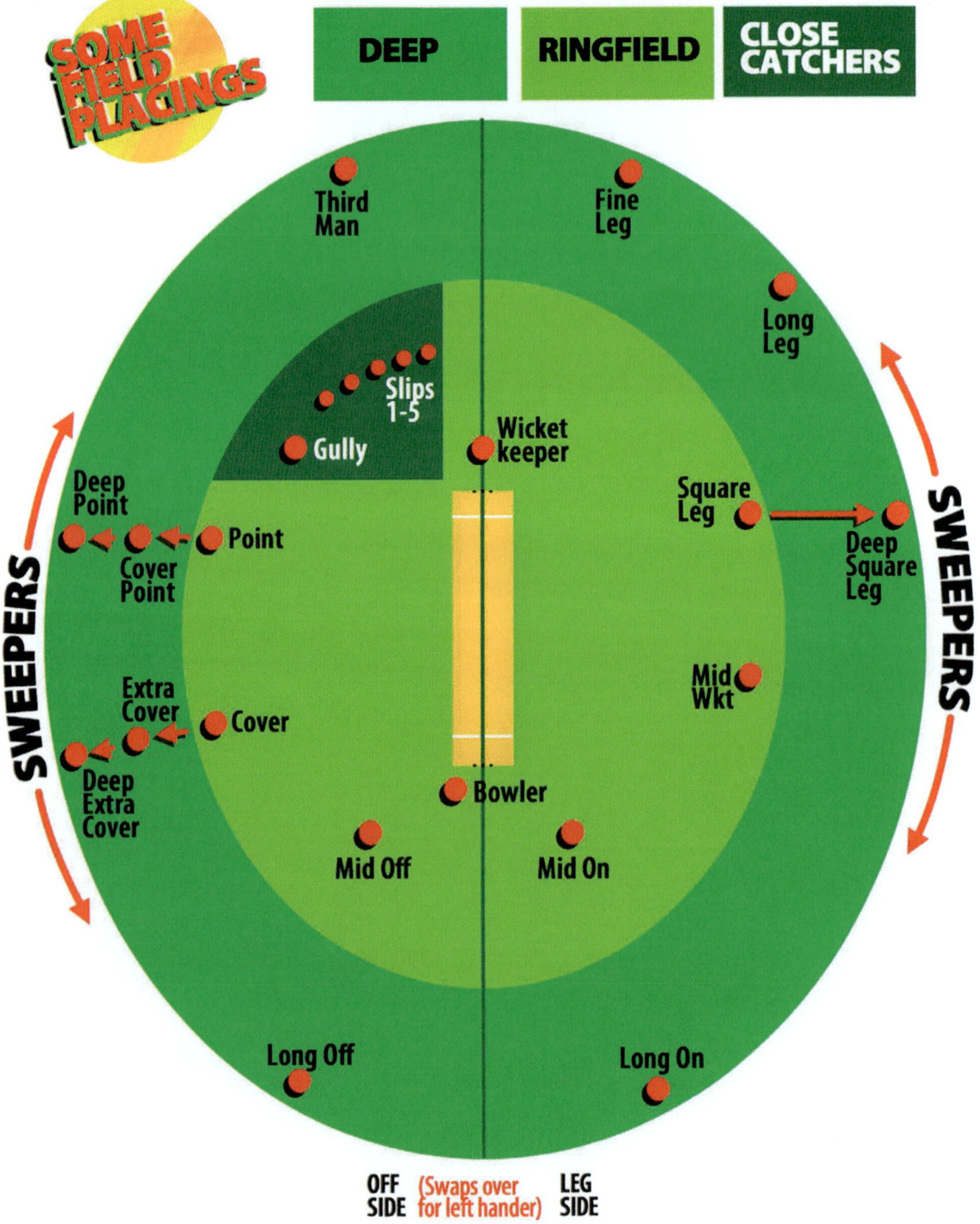

DEEP | **RINGFIELD** | **CLOSE CATCHERS**

- Third Man
- Fine Leg
- Long Leg
- Slips 1-5
- Gully
- Wicket keeper
- Deep Point
- Point
- Cover Point
- Square Leg
- Deep Square Leg
- Extra Cover
- Cover
- Mid Wkt
- Deep Extra Cover
- Bowler
- Mid Off
- Mid On
- Long Off
- Long On

SWEEPERS (both sides)

OFF SIDE (Swaps over for left hander) LEG SIDE

12

CLOSE CATCHERS
Here you need quick reactions and concentration. You need to watch the batter closely.
Cover the diagram and name 2 close fielding positions

DEEP FIELDERS
Here you are trying to stop the ball going for four or six. You need to take high catches and like all fielders you need to be fast and agile, but from the boundary you need an extra strong throw.
Now name 4 deep fielders

RING FIELDERS
These positions are about half way between the pitch and the boundary. Here your job is to stop singles, get run outs and look for catches. You need to be quick to stop the ball and have an accurate throw.
Now name 2 ringfielders

THROWING
Unless you take a catch the fielder's final job is an accurate throw. It can make the difference between the batter being run out or surviving. Which can make the difference between winning and losing.

A fielder takes a catch in the deep.
He has his eyes on the ball, hands together and he has pulled his hands into his chest

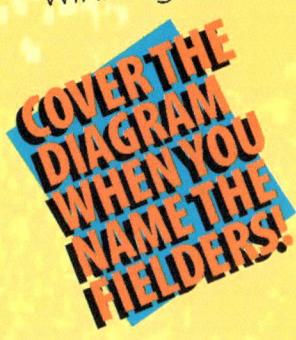

COVER THE DIAGRAM WHEN YOU NAME THE FIELDERS!

Good fielding can be match winning. Stopping the scoring, catching the catches, helping your bowlers to keep the pressure on or defending hard when the opposition batters are going well.

Throwing

HSEL- of course!

Fast accurate throwing changes the game. When you watch cricket on TV or better at a match how often do you see what should be 2 runs cut down to 1 by a rocket throw? And that can lead to a batter taking chances and getting out. A match can be won by a run out and the pin point throw from the boundary so often catches the most alert batter out!

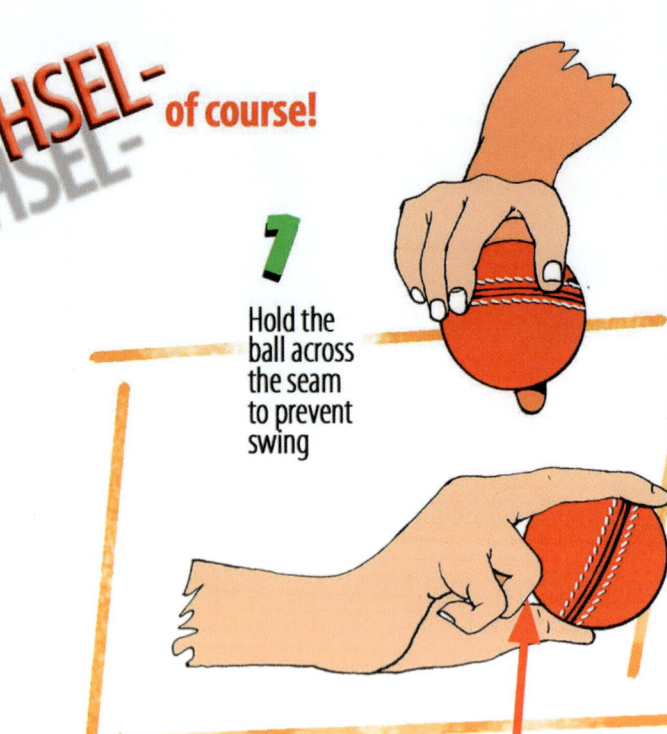

1 Hold the ball across the seam to prevent swing

Ball held in fingers — Gap

2 Eyes on target- back foot 90 degrees to target. Take a long straight stride with front foot in direction of throw. Point front arm towards target. (It's a good idea to actually point with the forefinger) Make sure your elbow is level or above the shoulder.

Non-throwing foot

14

Walk in & Ready Position

HSEL- of course!

If you are fielding in a deep or ring field position you need to walk in then get into the ready position. If the fielders smoothly walk in as a unit it puts fear into the batters, gives the bowler confidence, helps you concentrate and keeps the fielders working as a team. It looks good, the batters are less ready to take chances, it worries batters waiting to come in and makes it natural for you to move in to the ready position.

1 Walk In

As the bowler runs up, start walking towards the batter- 3 or 4 steps.

Light on your feet, so you are ready to make any sudden move, slighty crouched, eyes on batter, hands spread ready for action.

SKILL SHEET

HSEL

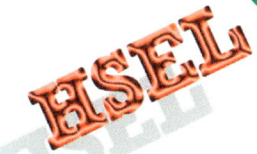

The ready position-think of a goalkeeper, tennis or baseball player-balanced, aware, ready to stop the batter taking a single, getting a run out or taking that vital catch!

2 Ready Position

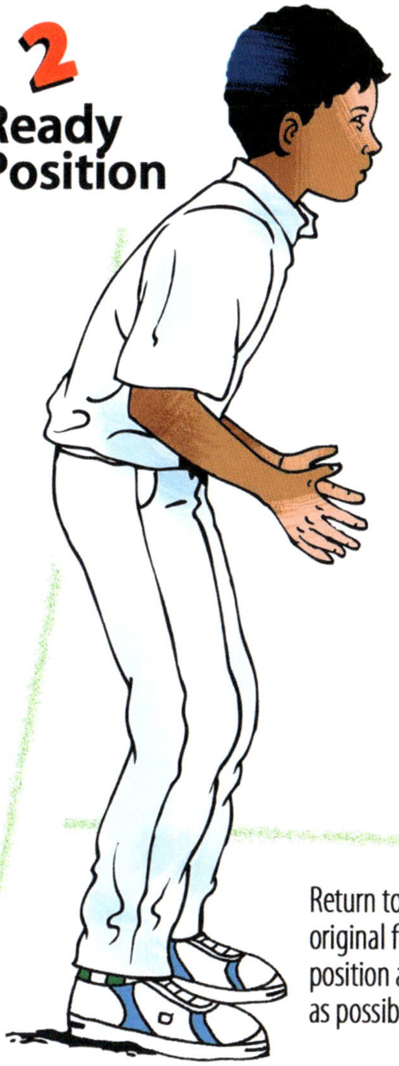

Just before the ball is released make a slight jump on to the balls of your feet. Keep hands spread ready for action.

Keep looking at the batter and be ready to move anywhere once the ball is hit.

Return to your original fielding position as quickly as possible.

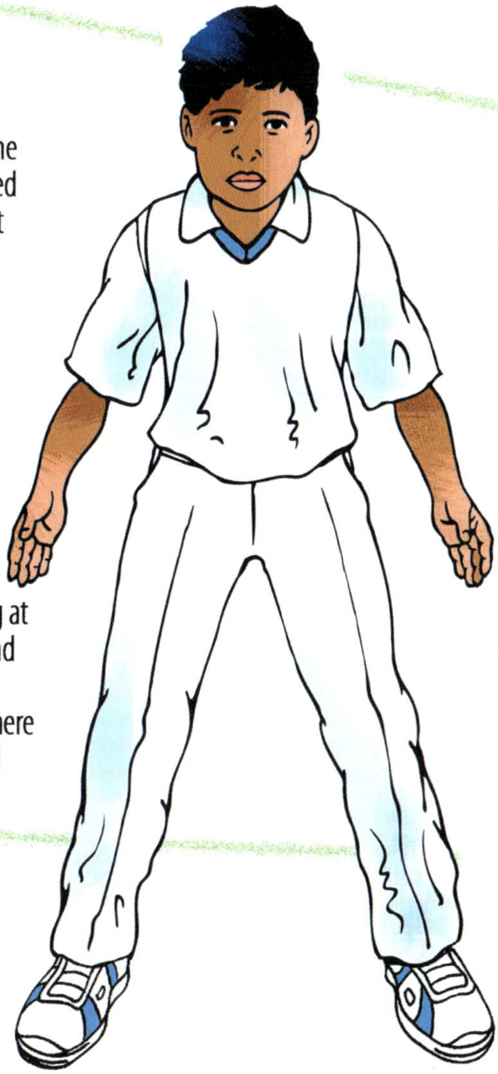

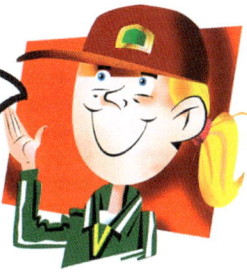

If you work on this you will be a better fielder. If the team works on this you will be a better field-ing team! So set an example!

One hand pick up & throw

When you are in the ring field (halfway between the batter and the boundary) and the batter is looking for a quick single this is the skill you need! Your job is to stop the batter going for a run or even better run them out if they are silly enough to risk it. You need speed, snap decisions and control.

1 READY POSITION

The ready position is vital for all fielders. You need to be slightly crouched with your hands in front of you fingers pointing down and watching the batter. Just before the ball is released move onto the balls of your feet, ready to move in any direction .

2

Watch line of ball and move at speed to non -throwing side of ball (same side as non-throwing foot)

3

Pick up ball outside throwing foot fingers pointing down and palm facing ball

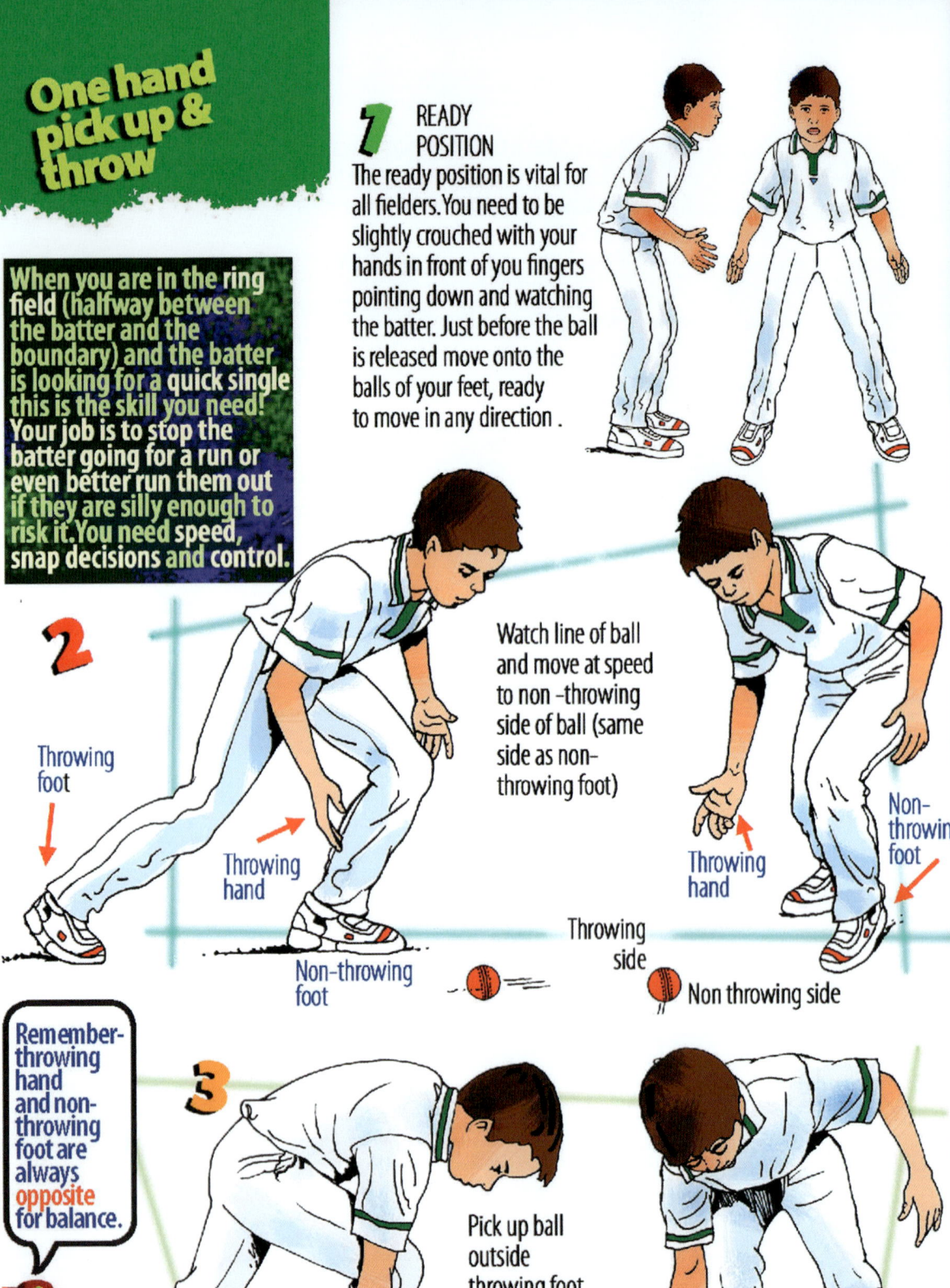

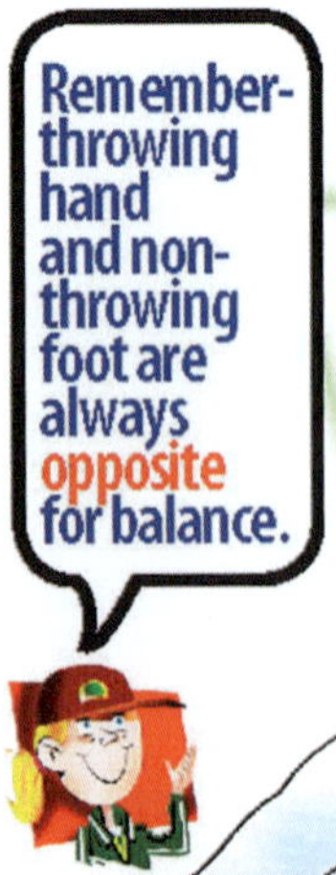

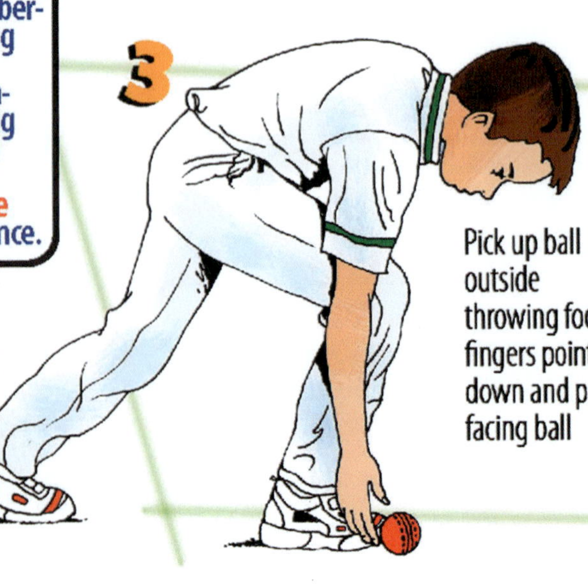

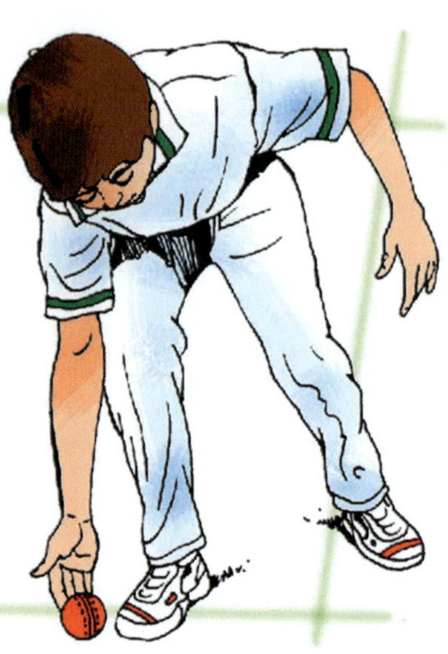

Go for a direct hit on the stumps or throw just above the bails into the keeper's hands.

Head moves up to look at target. As throwing arm finishes backswing point non-throwing arm at target

4

Finish with an accurate throw over stumps. Continue moving towards target.

OUT!

Make sure there is a fielder behind the keeper in line with the throw. This is called 'backing up'

HSEL!!!

Saves overthrows. Run **fast** to the ball then **underarm** to the keeper. You need a change of speed from fast to slower.

19

MORE ABOUT FIELDING

How to be really useful: keep your eyes on the captain between deliveries-he or she might want you to go somewhere else in the field-how can the skipper move you if you're in a dream?

1 Can you work out who this fielder is?
2 Where?

A little bit of practice makes you a better fielder. A **lot** of practice and you will be chasing after the ball, speeding it in to get those run outs, stopping everything and taking the catches. It's great to have the ball smack into your hands and see the batter walking off! And what a difference it makes to the whole side! The bowlers bowl better and the incoming batters are worried before they get to the crease. If your fielding is **good** you can win matches against sides who might have better batters and bowlers than you. So it's so much worth working at this. **Practice hard and you will enjoy fielding.** Just think about it-fielding is at least half the match!

When you get to your fielding position try lining up with something or make a very small mark so that you can remember the place. Don't drift off somewhere else-stay where the boss puts you!
How can the poor skipper run things if the fielders wander all over the place?

When throwing in listen for the calls, but you will usually throw to the keeper, the player with the gloves.

Keep the new ball off the ground, the bowler wants that shine kept on it!

Attack the ball! This doesn't mean kick it to bits, it means don't stand there and let the ball roll to you, but run fast to it.

P28-29 is the LONG BARRIER page. If you get this right you can be confident of stopping anything. Put long barrier TOP of the list!

5 What fielder is this?
6 Where on the field?

3 Can you identify these fielding positions?

If you get close to another fielder don't close the gap and get together for a good natter. You're on a cricket field, not in the park catching up on the latest gossip!

8 Here's a hard one. *Clue - what's the finger doing?*
9 What fielding skill is mostly used in this position?

If you're in the outfield (nearer the boundary) walk in two or three short steps towards the batter as the bowler is running up. Now you should be watching the batter to see where the ball will go. Always return to your position afterwards otherwise you'll end up sitting on the batter's lap!

4 Who is this fielder?
(Clue - a deep number).

A good fielding side can get wickets just by stopping the batters scoring - the batters have to take risks!

Work hard on underarm pick up and throw. So many overthrows come from a fielder hurling the ball at the stumps close in. Even the professionals do it!

10 What fielder?
11 Where does he/she stand?
12 What is the fielding skill in this position?

ANSWERS 1 Long leg 2 Leg side boundary behind bowler 3 Square leg & Deep square leg 4 Third man 5 Deep behind 1st slip 6 Fine leg 7 Deep behind keeper 8 Deep point on leg side 9 Long Throw 10 Slip 11 Next to keeper 12 Close catching

Retrieving the ball

You often have to run away from the action to collect the ball. While you're gone you need to be aware of what's happening behind you. As you are going listen for the call of 'bowlers end' or 'keeper' so that you already know what you should do before you turn back to the play.

1 READY POSITION
The ready position is vital for all fielders. You need to be slightly crouched with your hands in front of you fingers pointing down and watching the batter. Just before the ball is released move onto the balls of your feet, ready to move in any direction.

2 As ball is hit past you turn and chase it on a line to non throwing side of ball. As you catch the ball up start to lower your body, ready to pick it up.

Non-throwing hand
Non-throwing foot
Throwing foot
Throwing hand

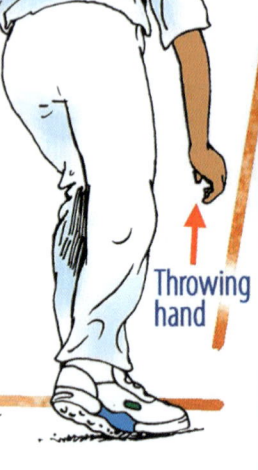

Getting low is the key. If you try to pick up from an upright position you will goof!

3 Slightly overrun the ball and pick up outside your throwing foot

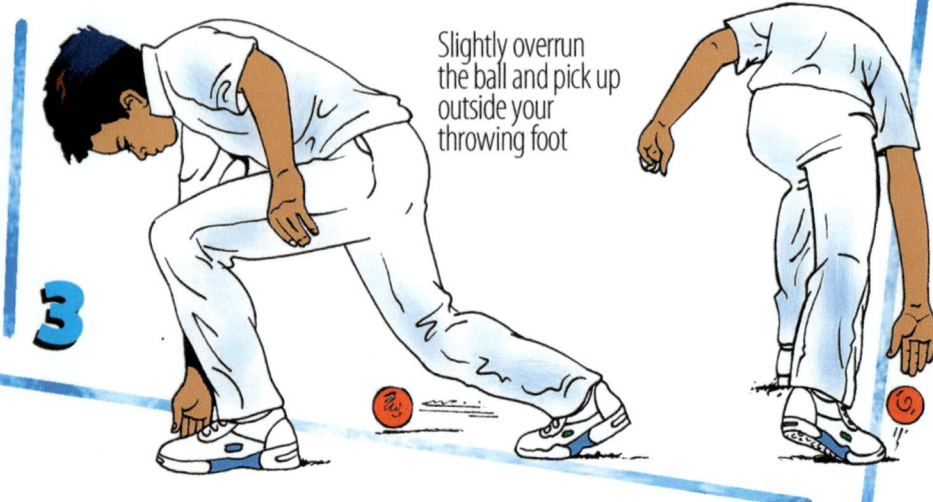

22

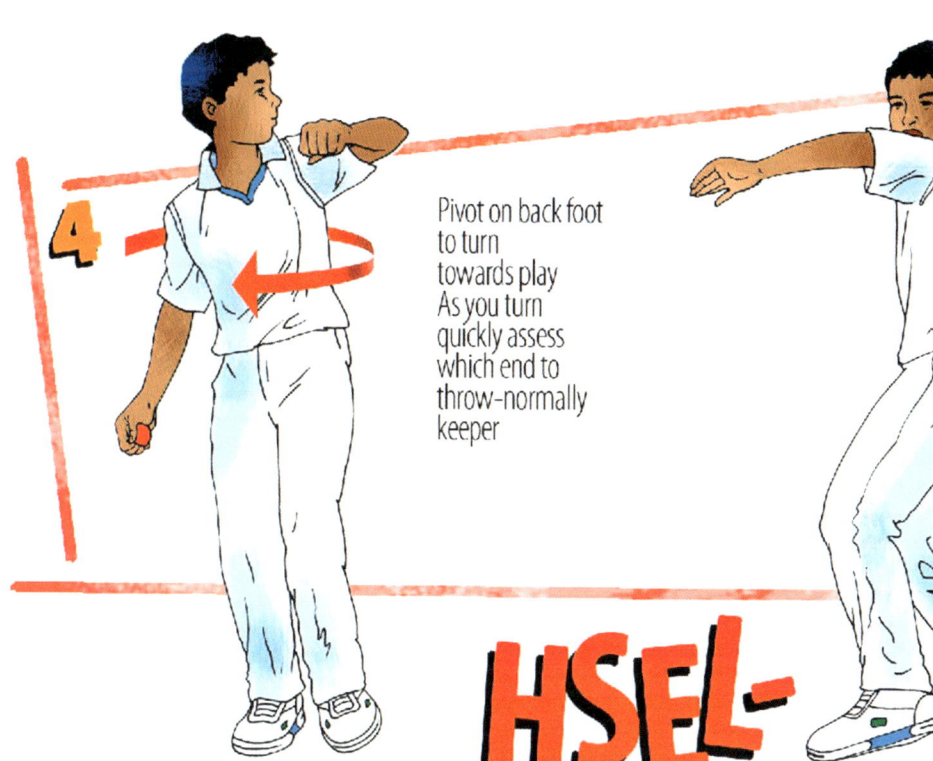

4 Pivot on back foot to turn towards play. As you turn quickly assess which end to throw - normally keeper

HSEL- at all times!

5 Remember grip - ball held across seam in fingers

Strong overarm throw. Front arm points to target. Throwing arm elbow level or above shoulder. Big stride forward for firm base.

Remember throwing hand and non-throwing foot are always opposites for balance

23

Crow Hop

I've never hopped that way!

The crow hop might seem too complex and difficult but it's worth working at because it's a great way of quickly getting in position for a long powerful throw, using your body's momentum. Next time you see pro. cricket watch the throwing carefully. Some form of crow hop is often used for throws from the boundary. Not all players do it the same. Some click the feet together, some pass the back foot in front- but most use some method of getting the extra momentum.

1 READY POSITION

The ready position is vital for all fielders. You need to be slightly crouched with your hands in front of you fingers pointing down and watching the batter. Just before the ball is released move onto the balls of your feet, ready to move in any direction

2

Watch line of ball and move at speed to non-throwing side of ball-low position

Throwing foot • Throwing hand • Non-throwing hand

Throwing side of ball • Non-throwing side of ball

HSEL! HSEL! HSEL!

3

Pick the ball up between your feet, side on to target.

24

SOME MORE ABOUT FIELDING

Good fielding is about teamwork. This means encouraging each other! If someone makes a mistake, what are you going to do?
Clutch your head and stamp the ground? Shout out 'Long Barrier!'? Stare daggers? **NO!** YOU might be next to make a mistake, then your team mates will be giving **YOU** the grief. Remember, **no-one drops a catch on purpose**. OK, catches win matches, we've all heard that one but if you shout and scream at a teammate how do they feel? **GUTTED!** And will do so for at least 3 or 4 overs. So for that time you're actually a fielder short until they get over it. Supporting each other means better fielding!

Good ways to wind up an umpire
1 Chatter away as the bowler is running up.
2 Loudly appeal for LBW from square leg, point, mid wicket, cover.
3 Move from your fielding position while the bowler is running up.
4 Constantly make cracks about the batters lack of skill.
5 Run up to the umpire and fiercely dispute the decision.
All these things will get you a steely umpire's stare and some stern remarks. (Might even get you chucked out of the match!)

Good ways to wind up a bowler:
1 The bowler has just bowled a wide-now is the time to shout 'on the stumps!'
2 Shout out some advice to the bowler just as she or he is starting their run.
3 Constantly roll the new ball along the ground, so roughing it up.
Do all this and you can forget that birthday present you were looking forward to!

Good ways to wind up a captain:
1 Stand around with hands in pockets.
2 Look anywhere else but at the captain between overs when he or she might want to change the field.
3 Don't walk in when you're in the outfield.
4 Change the field yourself
5 Constantly give the captain advice.
6 Stand where **you** want to, not where the boss has put you.
7 Refuse to go where the skip asks because you don't like fielding in that position, etc.
Do all these things and you will be just the kind of fielder the skipper doesn't want!

PLEASE NOTE: JUST IN CASE YOU HAVEN'T CLICKED, THESE ARE WARNINGS ABOUT WHAT NOT TO DO!

Another thing to work on – we've mentioned it before – *Backing Up*. Any piece of fielding needs at least *three* players. The fielder throws in to the keeper or the bowler. If they miss the ball someone must be behind them to collect it. This is called BACKING UP and every player should be watching for it. You don't want to give the batter *free runs*!

Pass the ball around the field ending with a gentle catch to the bowler–don't try to knock his head off with a wild throw from the boundary!

1 What's this guy called?
2 Where does he work?
3 What sort of skill? *(and don't say good with a broom!)*

4 Can you guess this fielder?
It's an off-side position
5 What skill?

In cricket you **never never never** dispute an umpire's decision even if you **know** it's wrong. It's a vital part of the game. When an umpire make a mistake you have to accept it and carry on. It's not like football where they all crowd the ref. No way!

ANSWERS: 1 Sweeper 2 Midwicket or cover boundary 3 Long throw 4 Gully 5 Close catching

Close Catching

Close catching needs red hot reactions. You need to be able to move like lightning in any direction. Throw a tennis ball or bouncy ball against a rough surface and try to catch it. Good fun and great practice!

SAFETY NOTE! Under 11's must never field closer than 10 metres from the middle stump except behind the wicket on the off side until the batter has played at the ball.

HSEL - always!

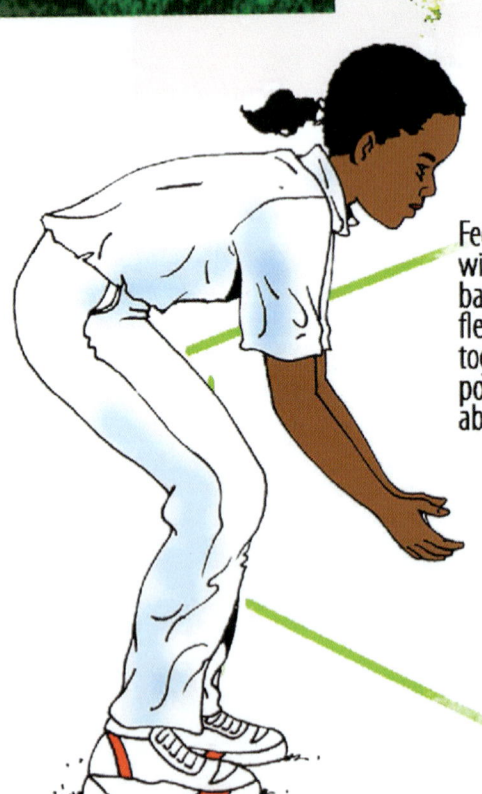

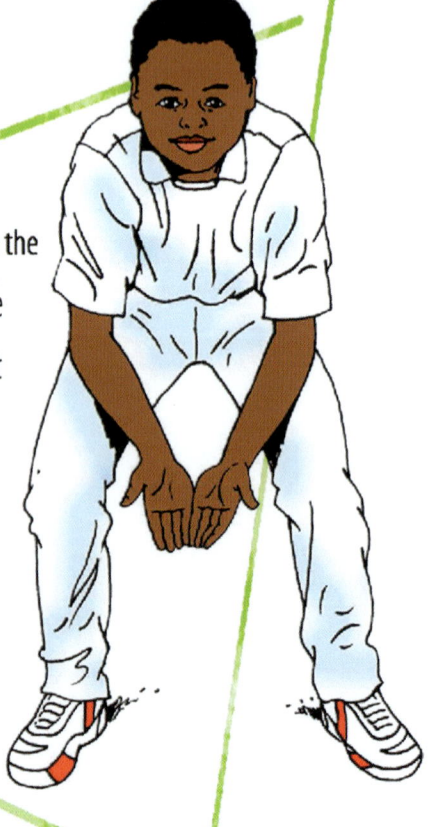

Feet at least shoulder width apart, weight on the balls of your feet knees flexed with hands close together and fingers pointing downwards at about knee height.

Eyes on the ball and hands out in front of your face

30

EVEN MORE ABOUT FIELDING

WATCH ANY INTERNATIONAL MATCH ON TV.

CATCHING - under 11's will not field close to the bat although close catching will be practiced at a club. Most catches you get will be in the **ring field** positions (about halfway to the boundary). Get as much practice as you can at this sort of distance-you can do this safely with a friend with a tennis ball. Work at it until you can pluck these out of the air like picking some juicy fruit!

It is so often a *catch* which makes the difference. A batsman is smashing the ball all over and gets a bit too confident. Suddenly the ball is coming out of the lights and the camera picks out the fielder waiting underneath it! *What if he drops it?* Or maybe you see the fielder roll over in the slips clutching the ball to his chest. *It's all over so fast you can't believe it.* People can remember great catches which have changed the course of a test series. Or the disastrous drop, letting off the world's greatest batsman who goes on to make a century and win the match for his side. Catching is one of the most exciting parts of cricket, and *we can all get good at it!*

CATCHING 1: Get in position quickly! What happens if you are not in position?

CATCHING 2: Keep your hands together! What happens if your hands are spread apart?

CATCHING 3 Fingers pointing down! What happens if you fingers point up or make a basket?

CATCHING 4: Watch the ball! What happens if you take your eye off the ball?

CATCHING 5: Relax your hands when you take the ball! What happens when the ball comes into rock hard hands? (Two answers)

CATCHING 6: Bring the ball into your chest! Why should you bring the ball into your chest?

ANSWERS: Catching 1 You drop it! 2 You drop it! 3 You drop it! 4 You drop it! 5 You get injured AND you drop it! 6 Good control 7 Trip to hospital!

CATCHING 7: If you get a flat (skim) catch always move your head to one side! Why should you move your head to one side? *Think about it!*

CATCHING 8: Celebrate politely with your team then clap the batter off!

C **8** Can you guess this fielding position?
9 Where in the field?
10 What fielder is opposite on the leg side?

1 What fielder is this?
2 What fielder are you exactly staring at over on the leg side? *Hey-you should be either looking at the skip or the batter!*

11 Have a guess at this one. What fielder is this?

3 Can you guess this fielder?
4 Describe his fielding area in two words.

12 Can you name this fielder?
13 What skill is needed in this position?

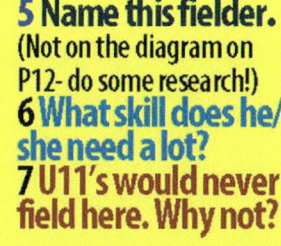

5 Name this fielder. (Not on the diagram on P12- do some research!)
6 What skill does he/she need a lot?
7 U11's would never field here. Why not?

Hey, we haven't said HEAD STILL EYES LEVEL for a bit! HSEL is vital in all these jobs!

ANSWERS: 1 Point 2 Square leg 3 Cover point 4 Ring field 5 Silly point 6 Close catching 7 Safety 8 Cover 9 Ring field centre off side 10 Mid wicket 11 Extra cover 12 Deep extra cover 13 Crow hop

33

Catching in the Deep

Fielding on the boundary is an exciting place-that's where you get the high catches-positions like long-on, long-off and deep mid wicket. The batter goes for a big hit and you see the ball like a tiny dot in the sky-is it a bird -is it a plane?-and you are underneath it. Practice these skills and you will be longing for the ball to come to you! Here are two ways of making sure you don't drop that vital catch.

READY POSITION

1

The ready position is vital for all fielders. You need to be slightly crouched with your hands in front of you, fingers pointing down and watching the batter. Just before the ball is released move onto the balls of your feet, ready to move in any direction.

ORTHODOX
Start from ready position below, diagram 1

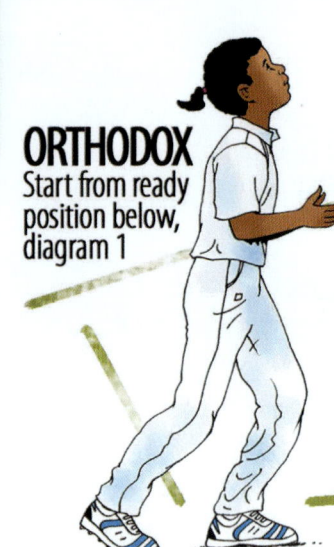

2
Move as quickly as you can, on balls of feet, to a position underneath the ball, keeping your head as steady as possible.

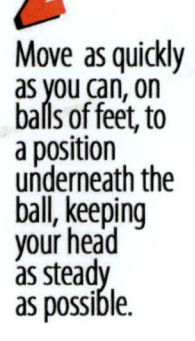

HSFL!

3
Steady yourself under the ball, bringing your hands together at or above eye level, fingers spread with little fingers touching parallel to ground. Knees flexed and hands relaxed.

4
Take the catch at eye level or just above. Close the hands round the ball and bring it in to your chest. Relax your hands as you take the ball.

Maintain firm base position

ABOUT BATTING

As a batter you are part of a team and your job is to score runs for your side, so that at the end of the game you have more runs than the other team. There are different jobs for different batters. The first two – the openers – need to get a good start

They will usually have to face the other sides' best fast bowlers. As the next batters come in they will have to score faster until the very last players are expected to take risks to try to get as many runs as they can.

There are times though when the opening players need to be able to score quickly and the last players have to play carefully to save the match!

This means everyone on the side should work on their batting and a good club will give you chances in all the different batting positions.

In the next few pages you will find some of the most important batting shots. Study these techniques and work on them so that you can bat anywhere for your team. Aim to be able to open against good fast bowlers and hit the ball hard as well if you are playing later.

Remember – batting isn't about *your* score, it's about what your team needs at the time.

EQUIPMENT

BAT

It's vital to get the right sized bat. Check this out – the top of the handle should be level with the top of your thigh. Get a light bat, pick it up and hold it out level with your shoulder with one hand only. If you can do this easily you have the right bat.

HELMET

Make sure your helmet is a comfortable fit, not too tight or too loose. If you're under eighteen you **MUST** wear a helmet when facing a hard ball. It makes sense – the ball is harder than your head!

GLOVES

Make sure your fingers fill the gloves but don't press against the ends. The gloves may feel a bit stiff at first but will flex as you wear them.

PADS

Don't buy oversized pads. The knee roll should flex – (where? At the knee!) If your pads are too big you will waddle instead of run and your bat will get tangled up with them. Remember! The end of the strap fastens on the outside of the leg.

BOX

Boys must always wear one when batting. Get a proper pair of shorts to support it. Your local sports shop will help you.

SHOES

Strong trainers with plenty of cushioning and spring are the best for cricket. Spikes are not essential

Grip & Stance

Get your grip right and you save yourself a stack of problems! It makes sense—if you hold your bat correctly everything follows!

1 Find Your Grip

Stand as if you're about to face a bowler. Rest bat against the inside of your upper thigh with toe of bat behind your back foot. Extend arms out

Keeping arms straight, swing hands down towards bat handle

Clasp the bat naturally. Left hand should be at top of handle, right at bottom (opposite for left handers)

2 The Grip

Handle held firmly but not tight.

Fingers and thumbs wrapped around handle.

Hands close together in middle of handle so that they work together.

V's between thumb and first finger in a straight line just to the left of the bat's ridge.

Bat's ridge

It's a good idea to practice the grip and stance until it becomes so natural you can do it without thinking

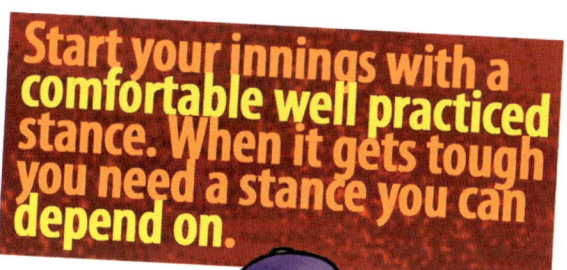

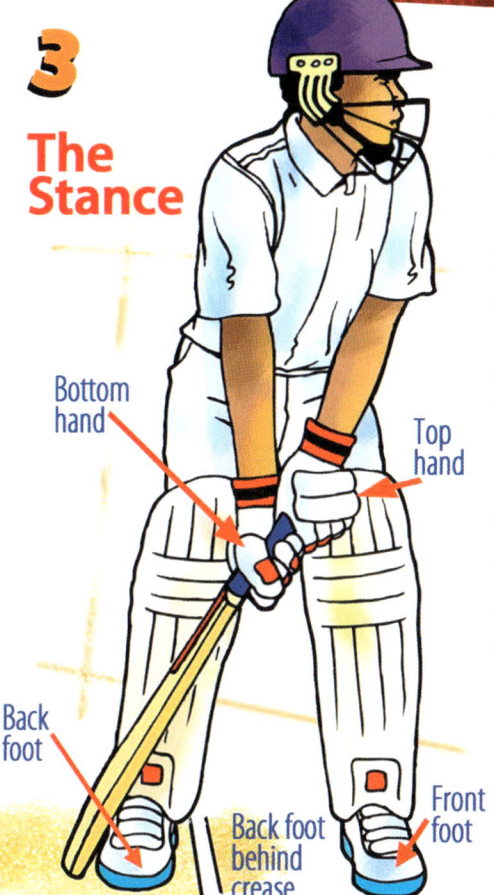

Start your innings with a comfortable well practiced stance. When it gets tough you need a stance you can depend on.

SKILL SHEET

HSEL!

3 The Stance

- Bottom hand
- Top hand
- Back foot
- Front foot
- Back foot behind crease

Side on to the bowler. Front shoulder can be slightly to the left allowing you to watch the ball with both eyes. Eyes level and over toes

Weight evenly distributed on balls of feet, knees slightly bent for quick movement.

Feet approx. shoulder width apart.

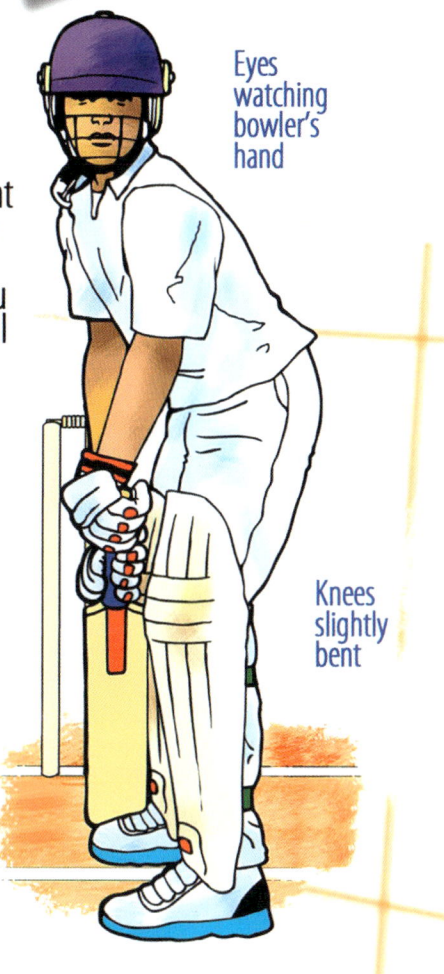

- Eyes watching bowler's hand
- Knees slightly bent

You're about to start your innings
Hopefully you've practised grip and stance so that it comes naturally.

The first thing to do is take a 'guard'.
The umpire will ask what 'guard' you want.

Hold your bat upright in front of the middle stump and say 'middle please'. Make a **small** mark on the pitch. This helps you know the line of the ball, helps you relax and tells the opposition you know what you're about.

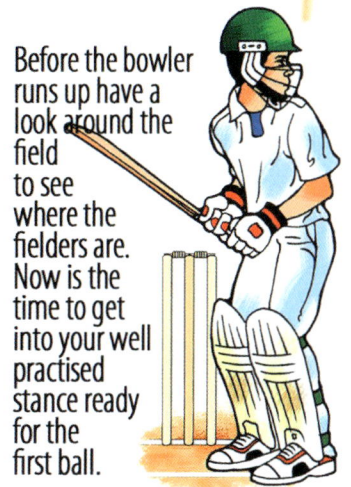

Before the bowler runs up have a look around the field to see where the fielders are. Now is the time to get into your well practised stance ready for the first ball.

39

Forward Defensive

Played to a ball landing close to you which would hit the stumps (good length)

1 Stance *see p 39*

2 Start in your stance
Watch ball from bowlers hand. Head still eyes level.

Bottom hand
Top hand
Back foot
Front foot steps towards ball

Straight backlift of bat. Head, shoulder and front foot move towards line of ball.

Length and direction of ball

Foot movement

Get this shot right and you can stay in all day–they'll never get you out!

You need this shot when you first get to the crease. At the beginning of your innings you're nervous, unused to the light and the pitch and you're not flowing. This is when the bowler wants to get rid of you–before you've got your eye in! But get through that early difficult bit and you can take over!

This shot is all about **control** and **thinking**. It's great smashing the ball all around the park isn't it? But sometimes your team needs you to stay there at all costs. This is where you have to use your **brains** and not play **silly shots** (like so many international players!)

SKILL SHEET

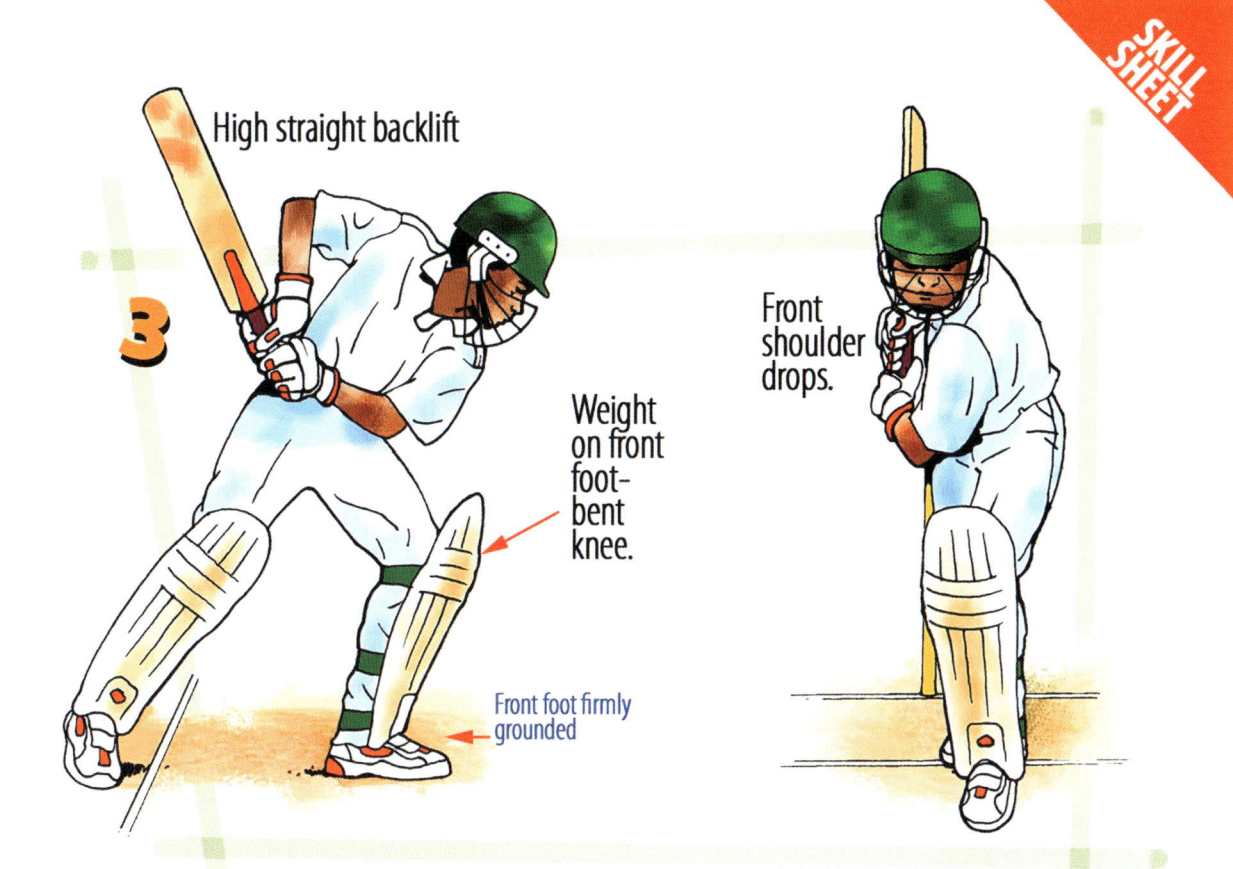

3

High straight backlift

Weight on front foot- bent knee.

Front foot firmly grounded

Front shoulder drops.

4

Head over ball

Straight back leg

Lifted heel

Eyes over ball- relaxed bottom hand. Don't push out at the ball- let it come to you.

Direction of ball

Aim to drop the ball just in front of your feet

Bat and pad together. Ball hit with full face of bat.

Back foot firmly anchored **behind** crease

Picture the ball going **down** on to the pitch and that's where it will go!

41

THESE BATTERS WON'T LAST LONG!

A

Can you spot what he's doing wrong with his
1. **Backlift**
2. **Body**
3. **Feet**

B

Can you see what's wrong with his
1. **Hands**
2. **Bat**
3. **Front foot**
4. **Back foot**

C

This is hopeless. Can you see the **BIG MISTAKE** he is making?

D

Can you see what's wrong with his
1. **Bat**
2. **Knees**
3. **Stance**

Clue: needs to turn clockwise

OUT!

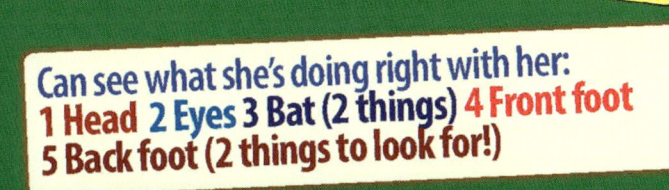

E Can you see why?

THIS BATTER IS GOING TO BE VERY DIFFICULT TO GET OUT

Can see what she's doing right with her:
1 Head 2 Eyes 3 Bat (2 things) 4 Front foot
5 Back foot (2 things to look for!)

Don't push out at the ball-wait for it to come to you

ANSWERS

A 1 Not straight 2 Leaning back 3 Moved back (should not move) B 1 Not moved 2 Not forward 3 Wrong way round 4 Well forward 5 Behind crease & raised ankle
C Bat away from pad D Away form pad 2 Not bent 3 Not side on E Raised back foot 1 Over ball 2 On ball 3 Close to pad 4 Angled down

Front Foot Drive

Played to a ball landing very close up to you. **(Overpitched)**

1 Stance *see p 39*

2 Start in your stance
Watch ball from bowlers hand. Head still eyes level.

Bottom hand
Top hand

Straight backlift of bat. Head, shoulder and front foot move towards line of ball.

Back foot

Front foot steps towards ball

High straight backlift.

3

Weight on front foot - bent knee.

Front foot firmly grounded

Now you've got your eye in-that is, got used to the bounce, pace and movement of the ball and the light and you're not so nervous, you can look to score runs. But as with all cricket shots this one needs thinking and practice. Sooner or later the bowler will make a mistake and overpitch (put the ball up closer to you). Now you can step forward and hit the ball very hard in front of you. It is one of the best shots in cricket and many international players depend on it. If you look at the drawings carefully you will see it's the same as the forward defensive right up until frame 5! The shot is finished with a fast swing through the line of the ball. Don't pat this-hit it hard-but don't slog! Practise your forward movement and the ball will race off the middle of the bat. They won't stop it!

44

4

Head over ball

Straight back leg

Lifted heel

Eyes over ball – relaxed bottom hand.

Bat and pad together. Ball hit with full face of bat.

Back foot firmly anchored **behind** crease

SKILL SHEET

5

Use full follow through if you can.

Bat speeds up through contact with ball and continues in same direction, finishing as high as possible.

Direction of ball. Hit between mid-on & cover.

Turn to P12 for field placings.

This shot depends on a **big** step forward. Once you get to where the ball bounces **you** are in control!

45

THIS BATSMAN IS THE BOWLER'S FRIEND!

1 What's the one **BIG** problem with his feet?
2 Can you spot 2 other awful mistakes?

EVERY BOWLER WANTS TO BOWL AT THIS BATSMAN!

3 What's wrong with the shot? *clue-look at the ball*
4 Can you spot 2 other problems with this batsman's technique?

46

BOWLERS DON'T LIKE THIS BATSMAN!

What is right with the
5 **Bat**-good
F_ _ _ _ _
T_ _ _ _ _
6 **Eyes**
7 **Front foot**

As in all front foot shots the **top hand** does the work. Hold the bat **lightly** with the bottom hand.

ANSWERS: 1 Haven't moved 2 Bat in air eyes not on ball 3 Acoss line to straight ball 4 Not got head down over ball, front foot not grounded 5 Follow through 6 Watching direction of ball 7 Well forward

47

Back Defensive

Played to a ball landing away from to you which would hit or go over the stumps (slightly short)

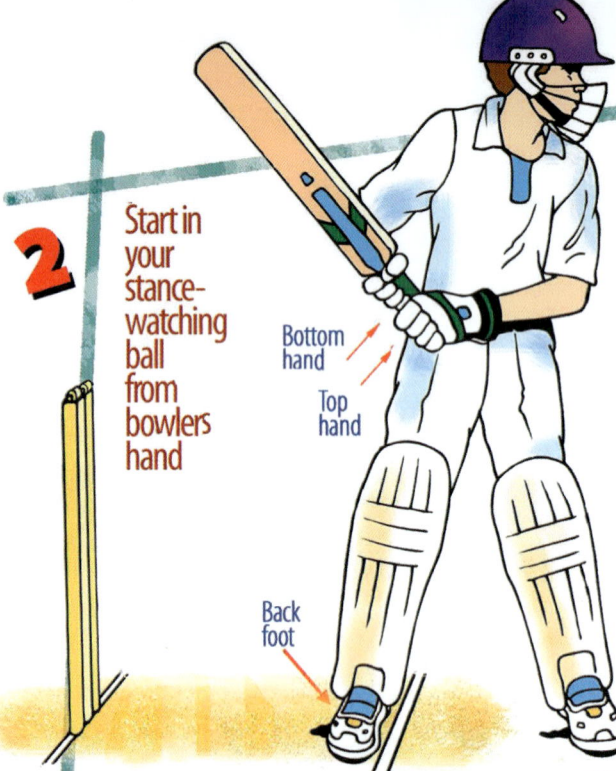

1 Stance *see p39*

2 Start in your stance- watching ball from bowlers hand

Bottom hand
Top hand
Back foot

Straight backlift- head, shoulder and back foot move back and across towards off-stump.

Length and direction of ball

Foot movement

With this shot they'll be wasting their time with the short stuff!

Another shot for when your team needs you to **stay there**. Don't give your wicket **away** (like so many international batters!). Another **thinking** shot. When the ball lands **short** you need to move **back** to give yourself a fraction more **time** to hit the ball. This takes a lot of practice but once you get it right you won't worry about the short ball. Work hard at it and soon you will be going forward to the overpitched ball and **stepping back for the short ball** just like the players on TV! The poor old bowler won't know where to bowl at you!

48

SKILL SHEET

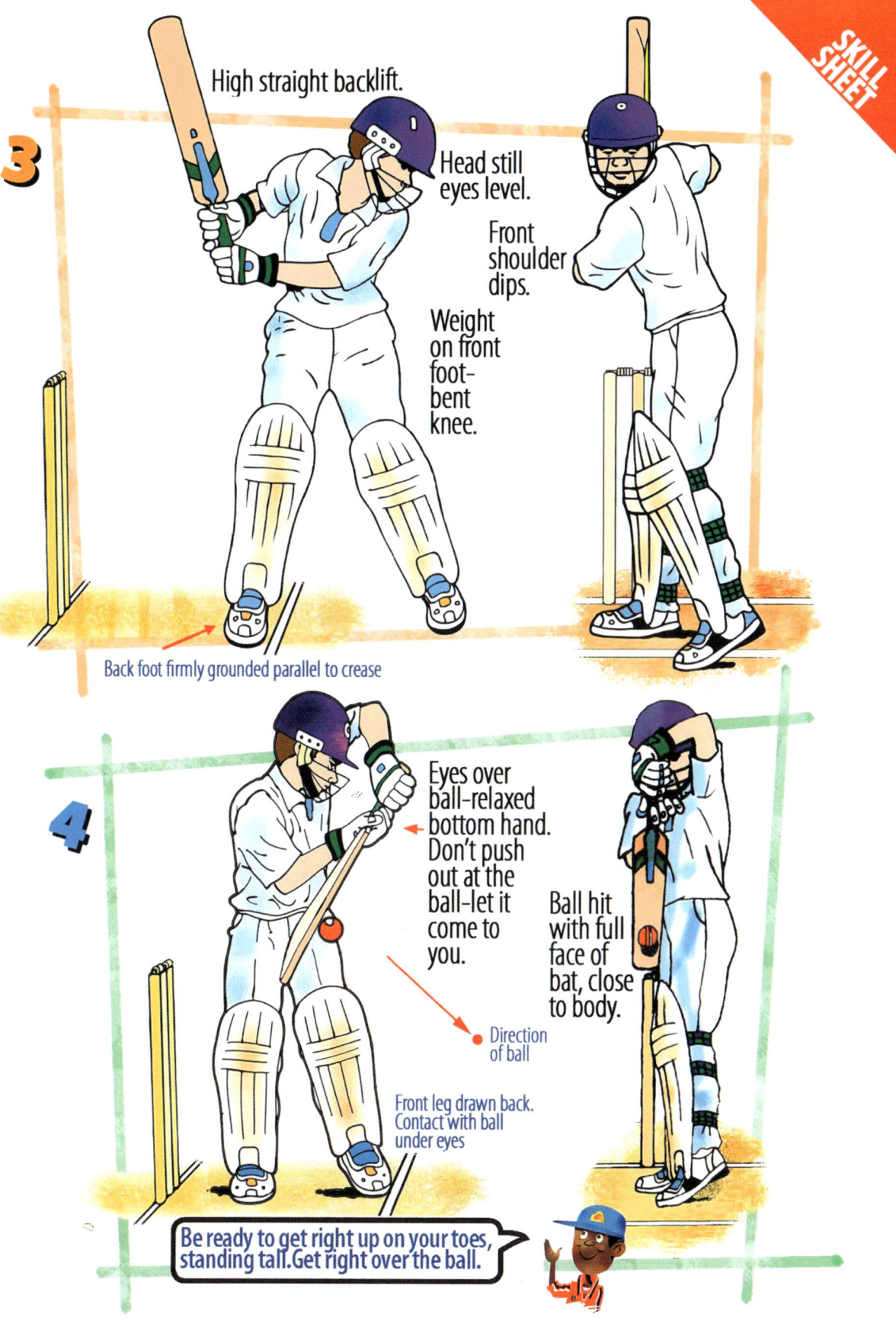

3

High straight backlift.

Head still eyes level.

Front shoulder dips.

Weight on front foot- bent knee.

Back foot firmly grounded parallel to crease

4

Eyes over ball-relaxed bottom hand. Don't push out at the ball-let it come to you.

Direction of ball

Ball hit with full face of bat, close to body.

Front leg drawn back. Contact with ball under eyes

Be ready to get right up on your toes, standing tall. Get right over the ball.

49

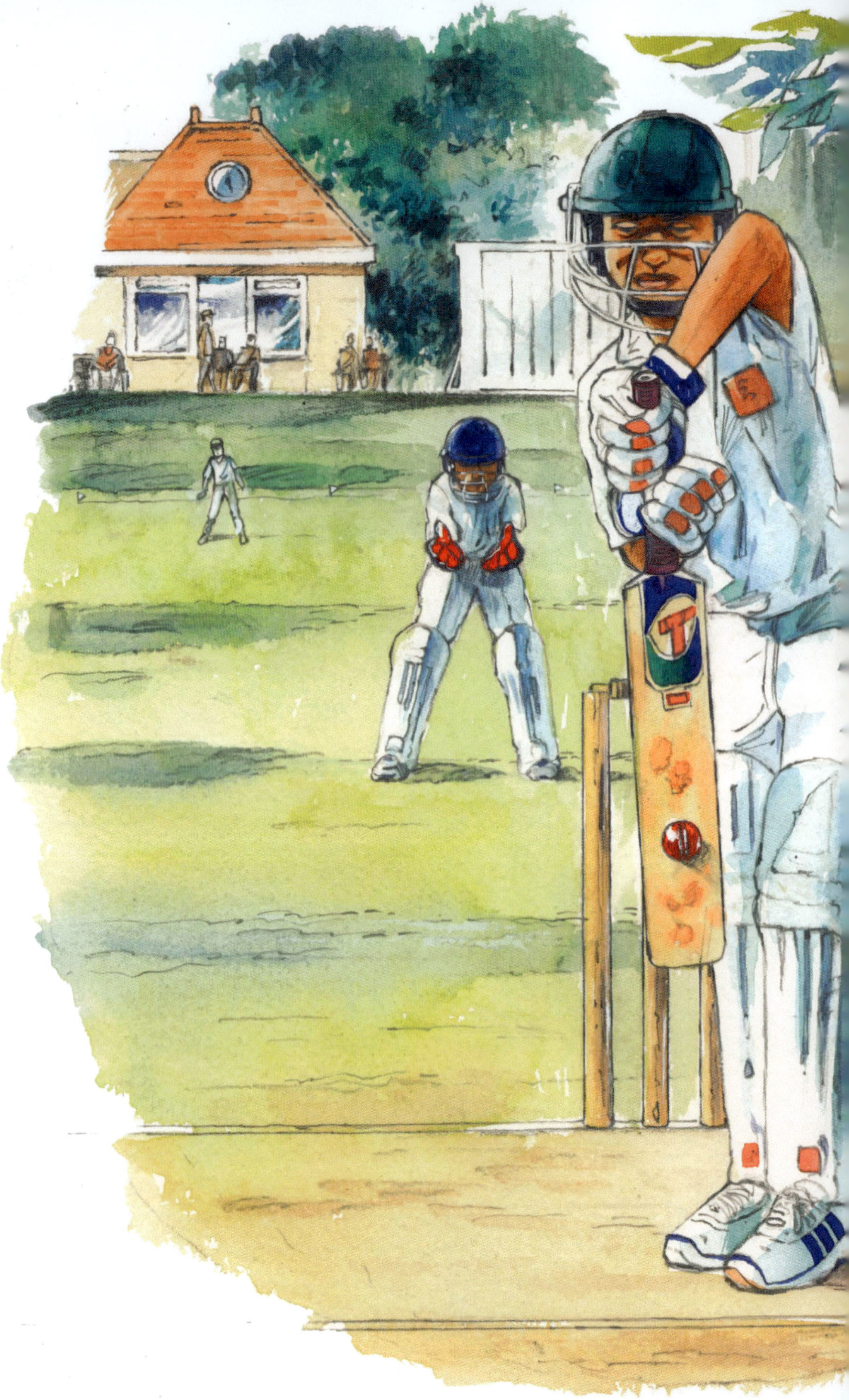

THE BOWLERS ARE FED UP! THEY'RE GETTING NOWHERE WITH THIS BATSMAN!

WHAT IS HE DOING RIGHT WITH HIS

1 ELBOW
2 BAT ANGLE
3 BAT, another point to look for,
4 BAT, one more point to find
5 BACK FOOT
6 What sort of ball would he play this shot to?
7 What would a fielder on the wicket keeper's right be called?

With a good defensive technique you can have confidence against any bowling. Good defence means good attack!

ANSWERS: 1 High 2 Pointed down 3 Full face to ball 4 Held high over ball 5 Stepped back 6 Short in line with stumps 7 1st Slip

Back Foot Drive

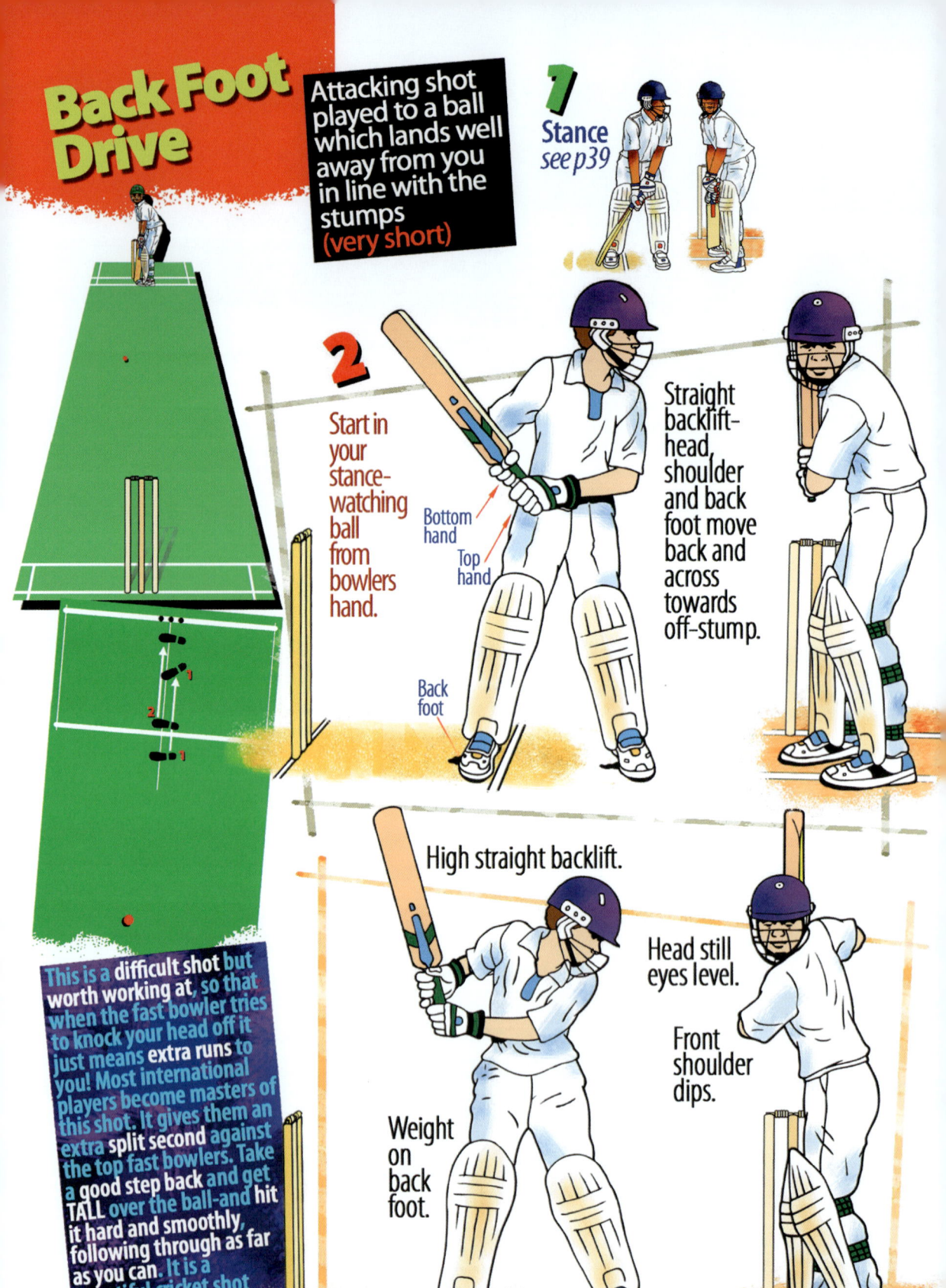

Attacking shot played to a ball which lands well away from you in line with the stumps (very short)

1 Stance *see p39*

2 Start in your stance- watching ball from bowlers hand.

Bottom hand
Top hand
Back foot

Straight backlift- head, shoulder and back foot move back and across towards off-stump.

High straight backlift.

Head still eyes level.

Front shoulder dips.

Weight on back foot.

Back foot firmly grounded parallel to crease

This is a **difficult shot** but **worth working at**, so that when the fast bowler tries to knock your head off it just means **extra runs** to you! Most international players become masters of this shot. It gives them an **extra split second** against the top fast bowlers. Take a good step back and get **TALL** over the ball-and hit it hard and smoothly, following through as far as you can. It is a beautiful cricket shot when played at it's best.

52

SKILL SHEET

4

Eyes over ball–relaxed bottom hand.

Ball hit with full face of bat, close to body.

Front leg drawn back. Contact with ball under eyes

5

After your shot keep your eyes on the ball in case a run is possible*

Bat speeds up through contact with ball and continues in same direction, finishing as high as possible.

Full follow through is best but you may find a lower follow through easier (check-swing)

Direction of ball. Hit between mid-on & cover.

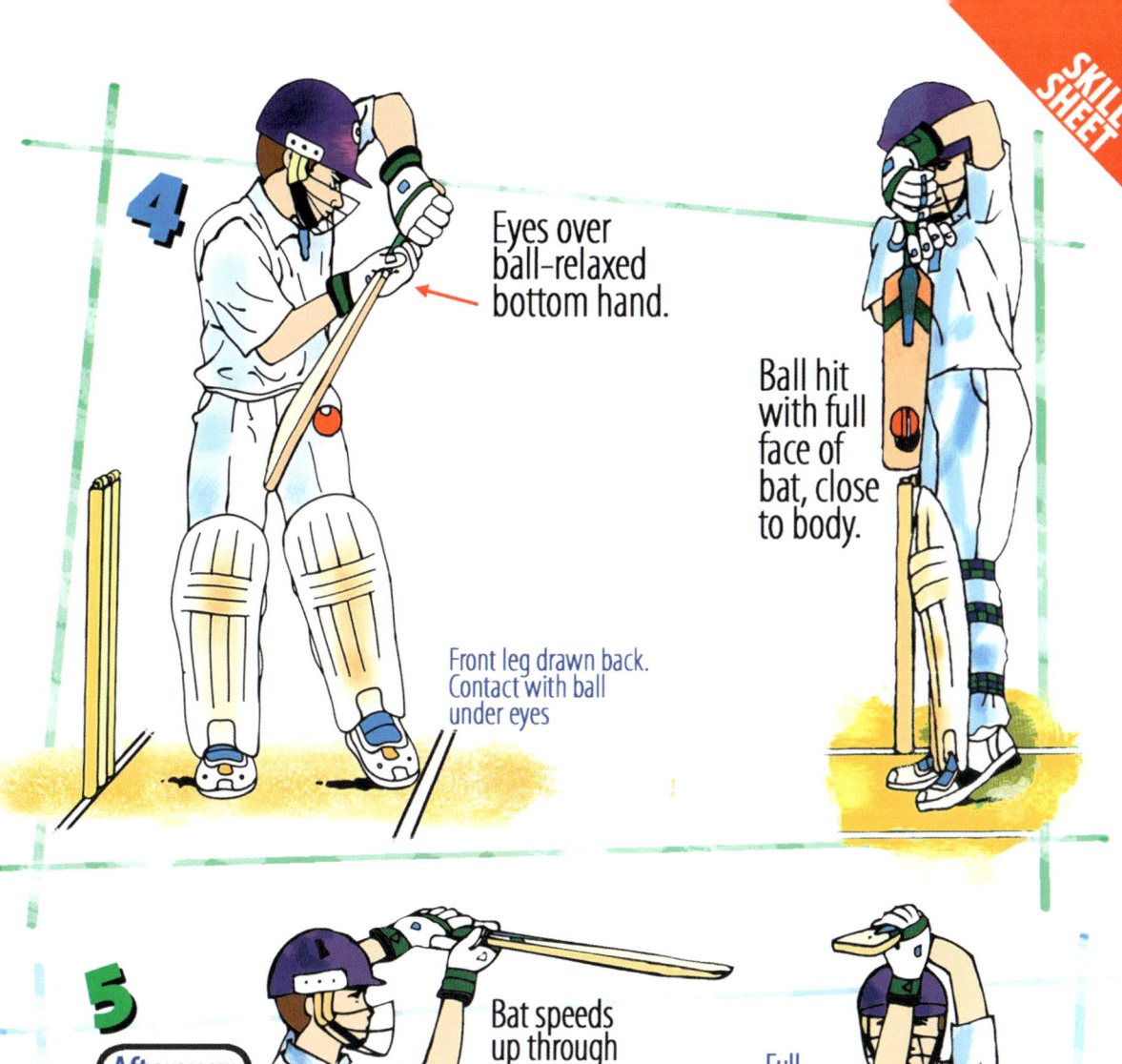

Turn to page 64 for details of running between the wickets

Turn to P12 for field placings.

BACK FOOT DRIVE Continued

No-one wants to get in the way of THAT one! (Unless of course you study the sheet of Long Barrier on p28 and practice it hard)

WHAT'S HE DOING RIGHT WITH HIS:

1 BAT
2 EYES 2 things to look for
3 BACK FOOT 2 things to look for
4 WHICH FIELDER HAS THE JOB OF STOPPING THIS BALL?

> Play the ball as late as possible. Right under your eyes when you hit it, then the ball will stay down. Play too early and it will go up – maybe for a catch!

REMEMBER— WHEN THE BALL IS IN LINE OR CLOSE TO THE STUMPS:

If it's **SHORT** play **BACK** (to give you more time)
If it's **GOOD LENGTH** play **FORWARD** (to get to where it bounces)

ANSWERS: 1 Straight in line of ball 2 Level & watching direction of ball 3 Moved back in line with off stump 4 Mid off

55

Square Cut

An attacking shot played to a ball short and wide of the off-stump

1 Stance
see p39

2
Start in your stance – watching ball from bowlers hand

- Bottom hand
- Top hand
- Back foot

Your head, shoulder and back foot move back and across towards the line of the ball as you start the backswing.

3
High backswing

Weight goes on to a firm back foot. Shoulders turn strongly away from the ball, ready for downstroke.

Remember – Head still eyes level and watching ball.

The bowler puts the ball short outside the off-stump. Now is your chance to **smash** the ball through the field for four runs! This is not a shot which you tap – it has to be hit **very hard**! Come down on the ball like **chopping wood** – and **hammer it**! It's a great feeling to see the ball rocket off your bat to the point boundary.

56

SKILL SHEET

4 Strong bottom hand

At top of backswing begin the downswing. Bat speeds towards ball. When you hit the ball your arms should be fully extended and the ball should be level with your body.

HSEL!

5 Finish with your weight on the back foot and a full follow through.

Direction of ball. Hit to the point boundary.

Turn to P12 for field placings.

Practice moving your **back** foot for this shot. Get that right and you can **pulverize** bad bowling!

57

FOUR RUNS!
Square cut continued

The bowler puts it wide of the off stump and the batter makes the bowler pay.

1 What fielder is getting their block knocked off with this shot?
What is right about the:
2 Back foot
3 Eyes

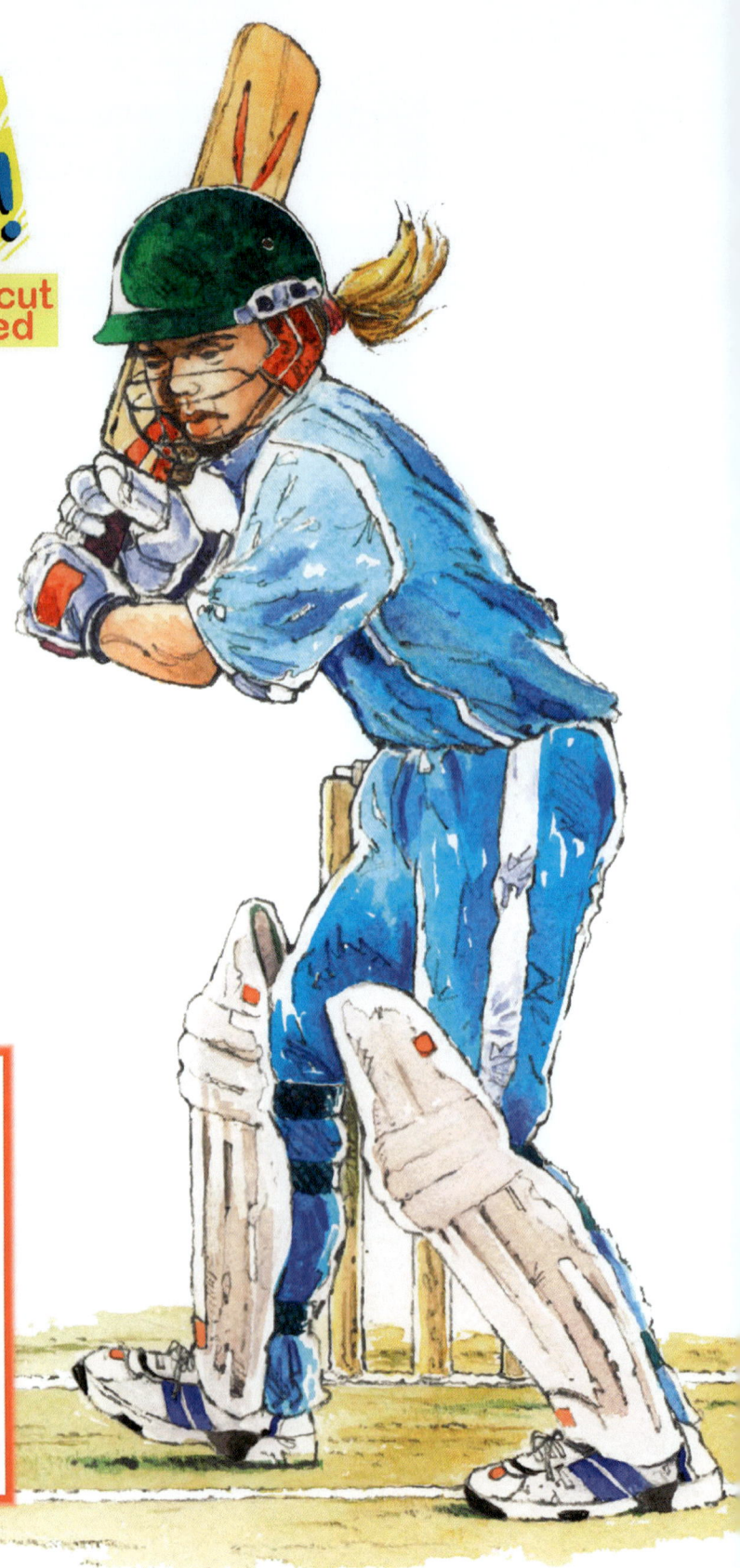

58

ANOTHER BATTER BOWLERS LOVE TO SEE!

4 WHAT 2 THINGS IS HE DOING WRONG WITH THE BAT?

THE SLIPS ARE WAITING!

What's wrong with the batsman's

B
5 front foot
6 Back foot
7 Stance
8 Eyes

It's the **bottom hand** which does the work when the ball is wide of the stumps

ANSWERS: 1 Point 2 Moved back outside off stump 3 Watching ball 4 Bat up & wrong way round 5 Stepping forward (should not move) 6 Has not moved back and outside off stump 7 Too upright (needs to be down over ball) 8 Not watching ball

59

Pull Shot

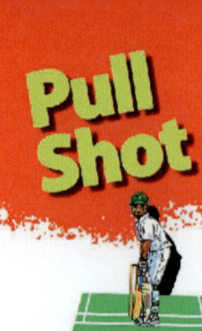

Attacking shot played to a short ball over or outside the leg stump.

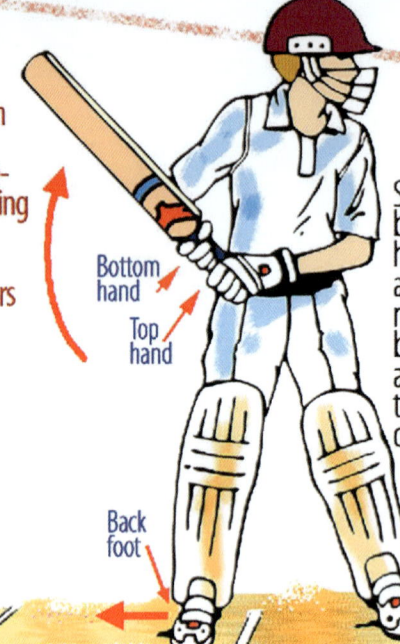

1 *Stance* see p39

2 Start in your stance - watching ball from bowlers hand

Bottom hand
Top hand

Straight backlift - head, shoulder and back foot move back and across towards off-stump

Back foot

3 High backswing

Head slightly forward

Your front leg moves back and to the leg side. Your knees are slightly bent.

Front leg

Remember - Head still eyes level and watching ball.

This is the most natural attacking shot in cricket. The bad ball outside the leg stump doesn't come along too often and when it does if you practice the foot movement you won't miss out. Make sure you really give it everything. You need to make the square leg umpire jump for his life!

60

SKILL SHEET

4 At top of backswing your weight moves to the front leg and your shoulders rotate horizontally. Bat speeds towards ball. When you hit the ball your arms should be fully extended and the ball should be level with your body.

HSEL!

Strong bottom hand

Front leg

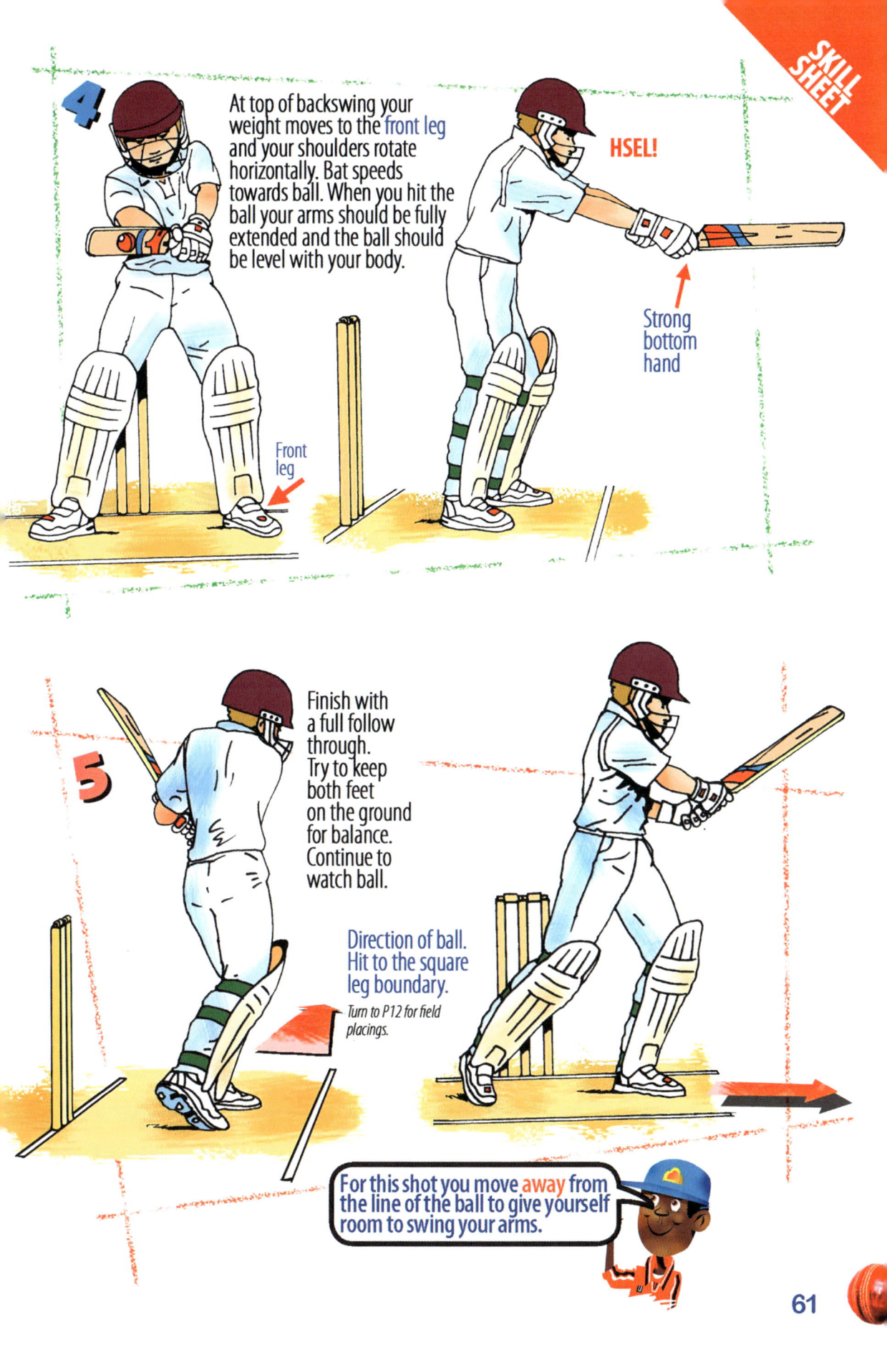

5 Finish with a full follow through. Try to keep both feet on the ground for balance. Continue to watch ball.

Direction of ball. Hit to the square leg boundary.

Turn to P12 for field placings.

For this shot you move away from the line of the ball to give yourself room to swing your arms.

61

PULL SHOT Continued

1 Can you work out where the ball would go without looking at a fielding position chart

No way is this ball going to be defended! This is going to the boundary!

What happens next to her:
2 Left foot
3 Bat
4 Arms
F * * * *
E * * * * * * * *

5 What line & length ball is this shot played to?

Eyes on ball. Good foot movement. This looks like four runs!

6 At what point should contact be made with the ball?

This is a dodgy shot if you don't get it right. This batsman was caught at square leg. The captain of the other side put someone there just for this shot and this batsman fell into the trap!

Can you see the mistakes he is making with his

7 Bat
8 Head
9 Eyes
10 Front foot
11 Body

The ball whizzing up in the air looks great until it ends up in the fielders hands-then you're walking off.

ANSWERS
1 Square leg 2 Steps back 3 Arcs down to point of contact 4 Fully extended 5 Short on or outside leg stump 6 In front of body 7 Going up not down 8 Up not down 9 Up not down 10 Leaning back

63

RUNNING BETWEEN THE WICKETS

STRIKERS CALL AREA

Non-Striker

"Yes!"

Striker

HOW MANY FIELDING POSITIONS CAN YOU NAME WITHOUT LOOKING AT A FIELDING CHART?

NON-STRIKERS CALL AREA

1 Why is it this way round?

ANSWERS: 1 Because you can SEE where the ball's going 2 Didn't run bat in on ground

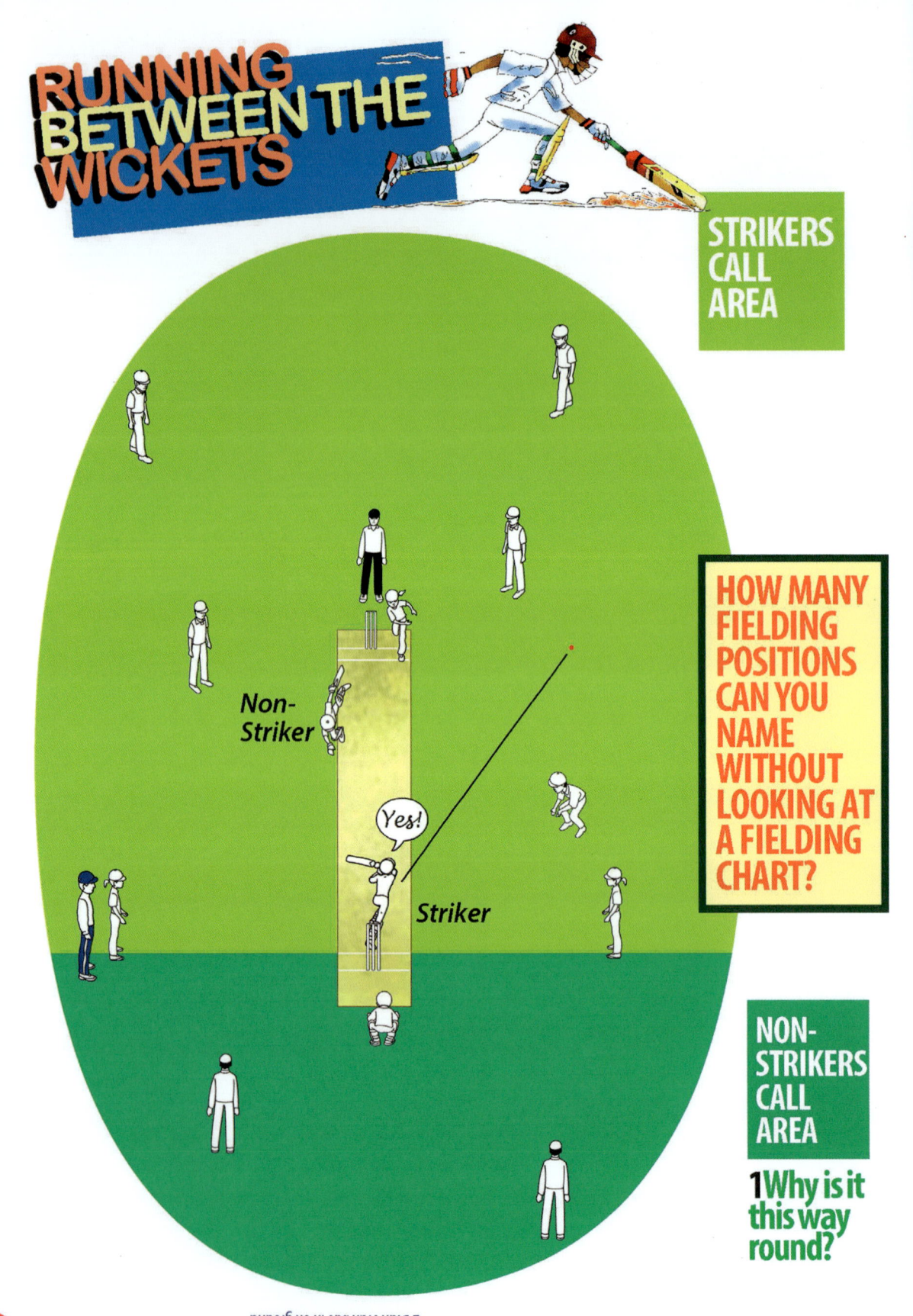

64

THE RULES OF RUNNING ARE VERY SIMPLE

Look at the diagram and you can clearly see the different jobs the players have.

The non striker is always the batter at the bowler's end and has the job of calling for the dark green area. The striking batsman calls for everything in front of him or her.

You should say 'yes', if you are sure of a run 'no' if there isn't or 'wait' if you think there might be a run but are not sure.

Imagine you're the non striker. Face the bowler. Get as far forward as possible keeping the toe of the bat behind the crease until the ball is bowled.

Then move down the pitch. Be ready to get back fast. Remember – loud clear calls! Don't mumble!

Once you or your partner has called called 'yes' go fast.

A metre before the other crease stretch your bat out as far as possible and run it in past the crease with a corner on the ground.

When turning for a second run always watch the ball even if you have to change bat hands.

If you can improve your running between the wickets you can easily add twenty or thirty runs in a twenty over match and panic the fielding side into giving overthrows.

If players work together and get a good understanding their whole cricket performance improves.

2 Can you see the mistake?

65

RUNNING BETWEEN THE WICKETS continued

WORK HARD ON THIS AND YOU CAN WIN AGAINST THE BEST!

LOUD QUICK CLEAR CALLS:

YES! NO! WAIT!

I think so, maybe... let's meet and talk it over!

DON'T HESITATE!

OUT! WHY?

ALWAYS BE READY TO TAKE A QUICK SINGLE

Run the first one *FAST*

IF YOU'RE THE NON-STRIKER

Keep the bat **BEHIND** the crease, facing the bowler, watch your partner and be ready to run at any time.

ANOTHER BATTER GONE!

do you know why?

WATCH THE BALL WHEN RUNNING

And always look for a **2nd run**

DON'T OVERRUN THE CREASE!

DON'T RUN INTO THE STRIKER

Pull up at crease, watching ball, *ready to snatch that 2nd run!*

ANSWERS: 1 Back foot not on ground 2 Bat not grounded

NOT

You've already run one, but there's another run there. **'Yes!'** you shout, watching the fielder and turning to speed up the other end. The throw is coming in, but because your running is so fast and you've been snatching so many quick singles the fielders are desperate to stop you and start throwing wildly–often you get overthrows!

OUT!

HIS BAT IS NICELY GROUNDED

Can you spot something else he is doing right with his bat.

Run rapidly and get used to making quick decisions!

Running the bat in on the corner

69

ABOUT BOWLING

The bowler wants to get rid of the batter and see her walking off! Also the bowler wants to stop the batter scoring. The bowler does the really hard work in the side, bowling accurately to make chances for the fielders. If a bowler bowls so well that a batter can't get runs they have to start taking risks. A run out can be the result of good bowling!

There are different types of bowlers; fast, medium, swing, off spin, and leg spin. All bowlers need to be accurate, and bowl a good length and line.

LENGTH

Length is the place where the ball bounces.

Why should you try to bowl ' a good length'?
- The batter is unsure whether to go forward or back and can make mistakes
- You get a chance of an LBW
- Good batters can easily hit short bowling
- The ball has time to spin and swing
- If you are a spinner the batter has less time to react

THE RED BOX IN THE DIAGRAM BELOW SHOWS WHERE THE BALL SHOULD BOUNCE FOR A GOOD LENGTH.

Under 11's should not try to bowl bouncers.

A *good length* is shorter for a tall batter and sometimes shorter if it is a bouncy wicket.

LINE

This means the **direction** of the ball from your hand

A good line is usually on, or just outside the **off stump**. The batter is uncertain whether to leave the ball or play it.

The best line can be different for different kinds of bowlers, but you should avoid bowling on or outside the **leg** stump.

If you bowl the ball a long way wide of the stumps the umpire will call **wide** and the fielding side will get a run or maybe two. This is another reason why accuracy is important!

OVER OR AROUND?

You bowl either **over** the wicket (which means that your bowing arm is on the same side as the stumps) or **around** the wicket (which means you go around the stumps and bowl from the other side). For left handers it's the other way round.

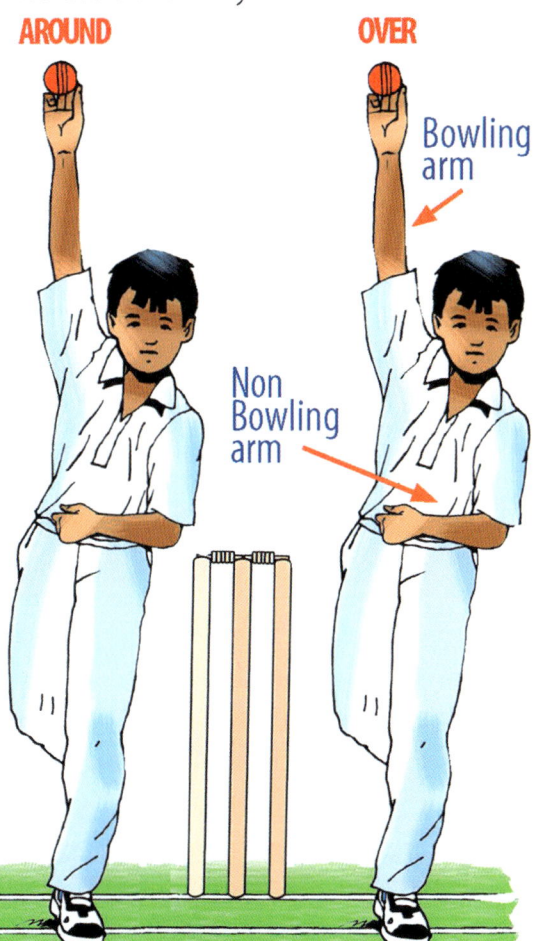

AROUND

OVER

Bowling arm

Non Bowling arm

What's right with her:
1 Eyes
2 Non-bowling arm

There is only **one** way to become a good bowler - **lots of bowling!**

1 Fixed on target 2 Flung out behind

71

Bowling – the run up & the grip

HOW TO WORK OUT YOUR RUN UP

NOTE: The non-bowling foot is always the foot opposite your bowling arm

1
Begin by putting the non-bowling foot on the front crease, facing away from the pitch

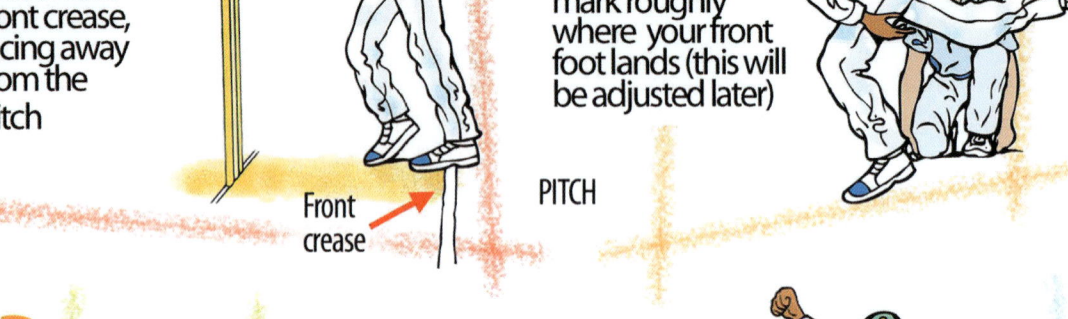

Front crease

2
Run and bowl a ball to where it feels right for you and get a friend to mark roughly where your front foot lands (this will be adjusted later)

PITCH

3
Now run from that mark back to the stumps.

4
Get a friend to watch where your front foot lands (make sure it's the non-bowling foot). If you step over or behind the crease move your marker until your foot is landing exactly on the crease.

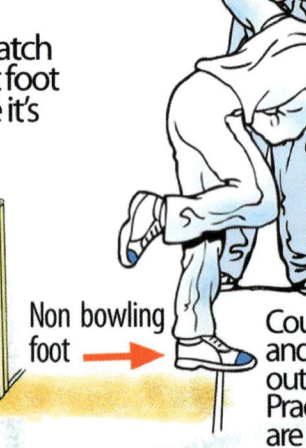

Non bowling foot

Count the steps and walk them out to your mark. Practice until you are landing on that front crease

WHY SHOULD YOU ALWAYS LAND ON YOUR NON-BOWLING FOOT?

If the foot you land on is opposite to the arm you bowl with you are balanced. Otherwise is it easy to fall to one side.

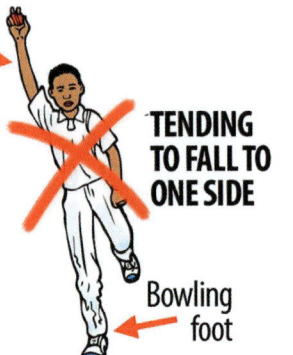

Bowling arm

BALANCED

TENDING TO FALL TO ONE SIDE

Non bowling foot

Bowling foot

BASIC GRIP - seamer

SKILL SHEET

The seam is held vertical with the index and middle fingers either side of the seam at the top and the side of the thumb on the seam underneath the ball. For full control the ball should be held in the fingers, not in the palm of the hand—that's how you get that wicked whip on the ball and get life out of a dead pitch!

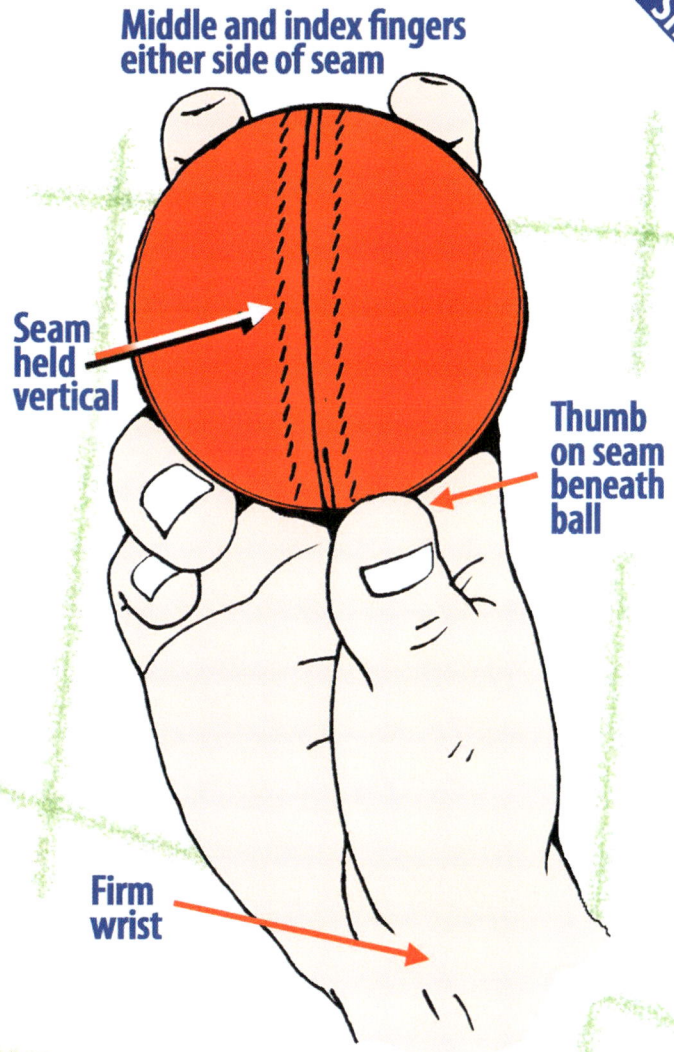

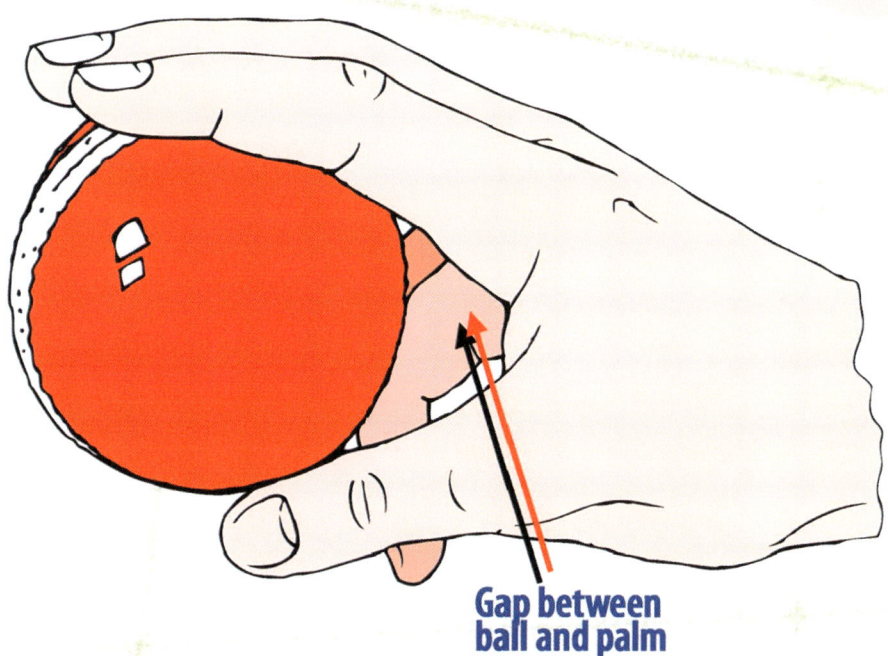

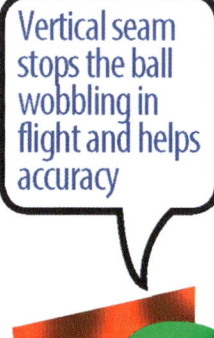

Middle and index fingers either side of seam

Seam held vertical

Thumb on seam beneath ball

Firm wrist

Gap between ball and palm

Vertical seam stops the ball wobbling in flight and helps accuracy

73

MORE ABOUT BOWLING

NO BALL

If you step over the batter's crease, the umpire calls 'no ball' and you have to bowl it again. The extra bad news is that the batter can score runs from a no ball but you can't get a wicket from it!

NO BALL 1 Your arm bends as you release the ball. This is a 'throw, not a 'bowl'.

NO BALL 2 The ball bounces more than twice before it gets to the batter.

NO BALL 3 The ball reaches the batter above waist height without bouncing at all.

There are three other types of no ball - find out about them on page 120.

Even more bad news about no balls

They cost your side one or even two runs every time, and that goes on **your** bowling figures.

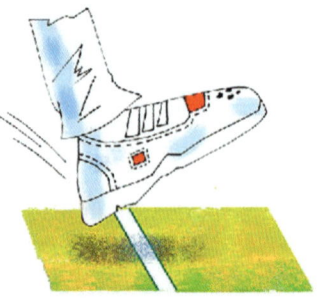

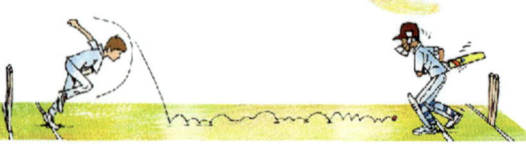

A Why is this a no ball?

B Is this a no-ball?

C Why is this a no-ball?

D Below: Why is this a no-ball?

RUN UP SEE P.76

Don't run up for miles - as few paces as possible!

ANSWERS
A Foot oversteps crease B No, foot has not overstepped even though it is in the air C Reached batter above waist height without bouncing D Bounced more than twice

74

Picture yourself in a tight glass box as you bowl.

"Hot in here!"

Your arms and legs are tight into your body and your whole focus is on the target area.

When you release the ball your arm should be high, at **11 O'clock**, with your wrist behind the ball.

Your arm brushes your ear

Make sure you finish with a complete follow through, still keeping head and eyes as level as possible.

You must veer off the pitch at the end of your run to avoid damaging the batting area.

Bowl at the top of the off stump. Keep your eyes on the target area.

OFF STUMP MIDDLE STUMP LEG STUMP

Reverses for left handed batter

Keep the seam upright Hold the ball firmly with your wrist behind it. Keep the wrist stiff. You want the ball to land on the seam to get some movement from the pitch.

SEAM (the stitched bit)

There is a lot more to learn about bowling than could possibly be put into this book. But **good line** and **length** is vital in any cricket from park up to test level.

Bowling- the run up

Seam Bowling

The next two pages show you the run up and bowling action. However you do it these things are always vital:
Make your run up as straight and simple as possible- no hops & skips and changes of direction along the way. Keep a tight shape and keep your eyes fixed on the target-usually on or outside off-stump. Don't run up for miles, take as few steps as you can. Run up smoothly and speed up as you reach delivery point. The whole point is to knock those stumps over!

1 Start of run up

Bowling arm
Non bowling foot

- Smooth and balanced
- Small steps to start
- The body leans forward
- Arms stay close to body above waist

2 Approach

- Continuing smooth and balanced approach
- Larger strides as you move into run
- The body leans forward
- Arms stay close to body
- Avoid skips and hops

3 Bound

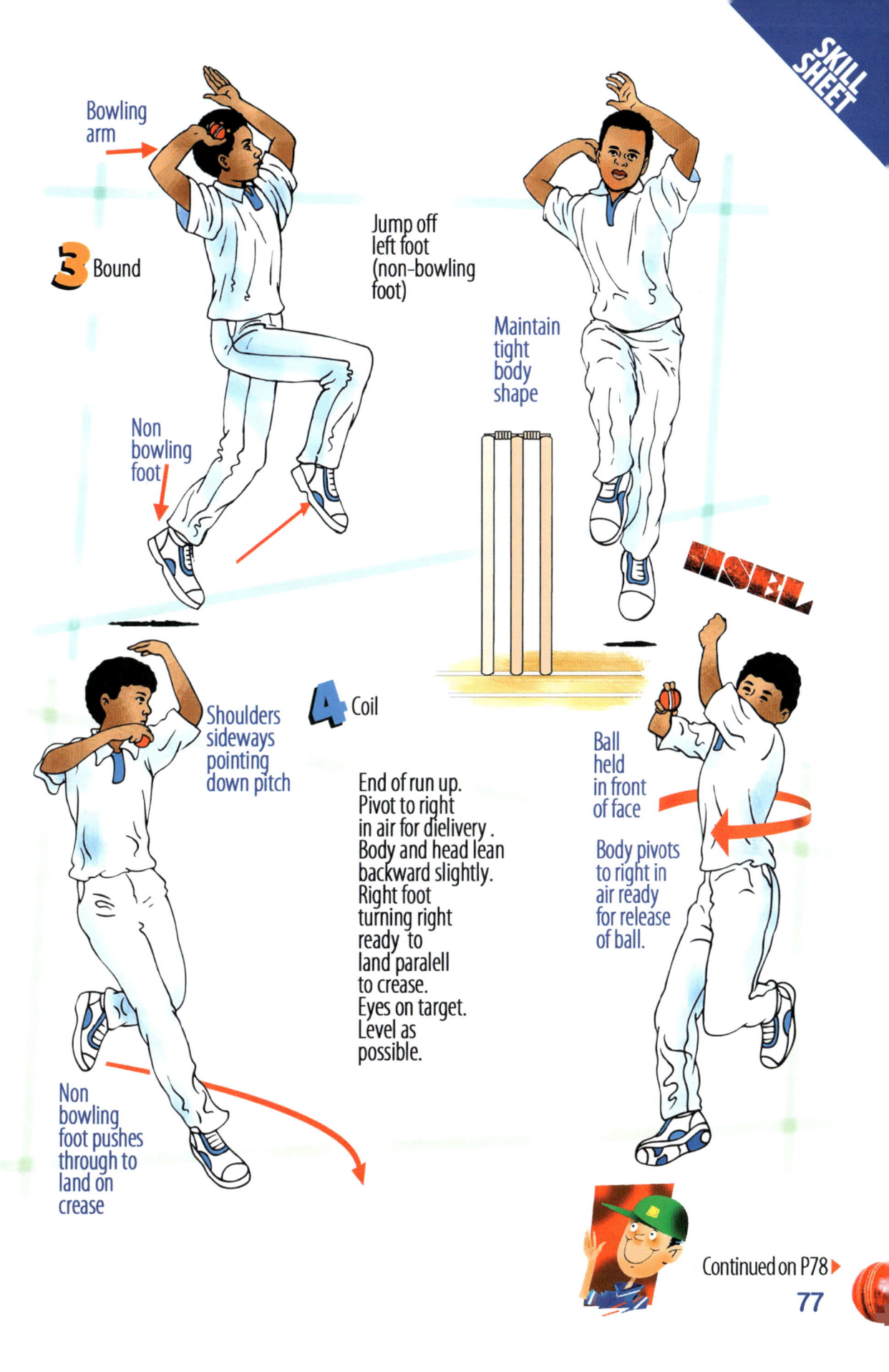

Bowling arm

Jump off left foot (non-bowling foot)

Non bowling foot

Maintain tight body shape

4 Coil

Shoulders sideways pointing down pitch

End of run up. Pivot to right in air for dielivery. Body and head lean backward slightly. Right foot turning right ready to land paralell to crease. Eyes on target. Level as possible.

Ball held in front of face

Body pivots to right in air ready for release of ball.

Non bowling foot pushes through to land on crease

SKILL SHEET

Continued on P78 ▶

Bowling
Continued from P77

This is the correct bowling action, but if you can bowl accurately and take wickets your own way - don't change!

You may not be able to keep eyes level during the whole of a bowling action but it is a good aim - **eyes level as possible head still as possible!**

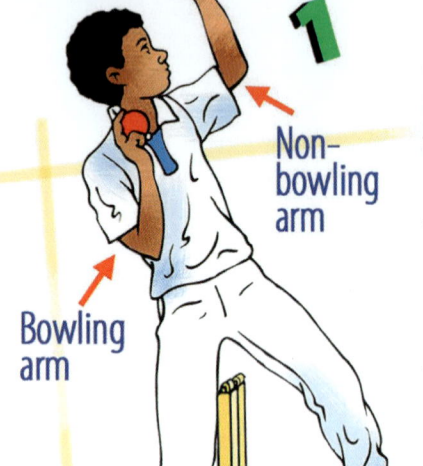

1

Your right foot lands parallel to the crease, non bowling foot towards target, keeping your hips and shoulders in line. Hold the ball in to chest with firm wrist.

- Non-bowling arm
- Bowling arm
- Bowling foot
- Non-bowling foot

Looking over shoulder at target

Arms & legs tight in to body

2

Push your non-bowling arm out towards target, bowling arm out and down

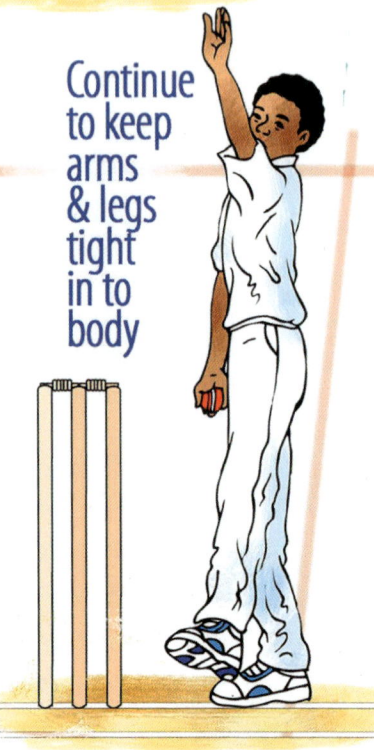

Continue to keep arms & legs tight in to body

78

SKILL SHEET

3

Bowling arm straight during delivery

Now your bowling arm swings up to a high release point. Arm should be as high as possible and close to head (brushing ear)

HSEL as possible!

Non bowling foot lands on or behind crease or it is a no-ball

High release point

Hand firmly behind ball

Maintain tight body shape

Non bowling arm tight into body

4

Non - bowling arm thrown out to give momentum

Bowling arm swings across body with a strong shoulder rotation. Right leg drives through.

HSEL!

Eyes remain on target

After bowling move off pitch to avoid damage

Keep it it simple! Aim at the **top of the off stump.**

79

YOU WON'T ALWAYS GET IT RIGHT AT FIRST

1 What does the umpire's signal mean?

2 What's wrong with this ball?

The bowler has got everything right. Good length and direction and the batter has lost the off stump. The umpire doesn't need to signal. No doubt about that one!
Which is the off stump?

If you find it easier to bowl around the wicket do so- the most important thing in bowling is accuracy-line and length

3 Look at the bowler: Around or Over?

SOMETIMES YOU WILL BOWL WELL AND NOT GET WICKETS

Bad ball, bad shot, four runs. It happens!

Only practice makes you a good bowler. It's not magic. It's not built in. It's practice!

ANSWERS 1 No-ball 2 Wide 3 Over 4 To a left hander (if you are a right handed bowler)

81

ABOUT SWING BOWLING

There are two basic types of swing, out swing which goes away from the batter and **in-swing** which comes into the batter. Simple!

SWING: Not an old fashioned jazz tune-

-not dangling a ball from a bit of string like a conker! Not something you go upside down on in a park! Swing is the ball moving in the air after it leaves the bowler's hand.

Practice bowling swing with a tennis ball with shiny tape on one side.

A ball swings when it's been used a bit (the 'old' ball) if you polish up one side to make it shiny.

ANSWERS 1 Overpitched 2 Off side close to where bowler starts run up 3 A slip fielder 4 LBW

82

The ball swings in the opposite direction the shiny side points, so to make the ball swing out, away from the batter point the shiny side towards the batter.

To make the ball swing in, towards the batter, point the shiny side away from the batter. It's that simple!

But the next bit isn't so easy-getting control. You need to make the ball swing as close up to the batter as possible (known as 'late swing') or the batter will see what's happening and put the ball away for four or leave it. You have to make the batter play the ball. And how are you going to do that?

PRACTICE, PRACTICE, PRACTICE!

Imagine you are a batsman and you see the ball coming towards you- just right for you to drive**(1)** through mid off**(2)**. You step forward, playing down the line as you have been taught and at the last minute the ball swerves away from you and snicks the edge of your bat for you to be caught at? **(3)** Of all the rotten tricks! Or it moves into you, nastily avoids your bat, smacks you on your pads and you see the umpire's finger go up!**(4)** Is it fair? But imagine you're the bowler! At last you've got your revenge on the batters who get all the glory! And by working on that swinging ball you'll be swinging as a bowler, sending those batters back where they belong, in the pavilion!

We were in a good mood doing this bit so here are some really easy questions:

1 What sort of ball would you drive? (One word)

2 Where in the field is mid off?

3 Which fielder would take the catch?

4 How was the batter out the second time?

83

Outswing Bowling

This is the **side-on action** - the **front on action** is shown on pages 86-87

Every player can swing the ball! Look at the drawing. Point the **rough side** away from the batter and that is the way the ball will go! Of course to swing it how **YOU** want it to go needs practice. One of the most important things is an upright seam and as the ball leaves your hand the seam should stay upright. Not easy! But with practice and experimentation you can get it right and then you will be a **dangerous bowler**.

Shiny side

Upright seam

HSEL - what else did you think we were going to say?

1 BACK FOOT LANDS ON CREASE

Wrist stiff

Bowling arm

Back foot (bowling foot) parallel to bowling crease. Eyes on target.

Non-bowling foot

Bowling foot

Extra turn of shoulders to left

2 DELIVERY STRIDE

Bowl close to the stumps

To a left handed batter this would be in-swing

84

SKILL SHEET

Get your bowling arm really high!

Keep the wrist stiff and the fingers behind the ball for as long as possible

3
RELEASE OF BALL

HSEL - of course!

Compact body shape

Every expert has a different idea of why the ball swings. Some people say it's the weather - but a study has shown the ball will swing in all conditions - and anyone who plays indoor cricket knows how much it swings indoors. Some bowlers swing the ball with a brand new ball which is equally shiny on both sides! The most important thing is to keep an upright seam and work on good technique and line and length - then you will make the ball swing - your way! Control is everything!

Fling the non bowling arm high in the follow through

4
FOLLOW THROUGH

Let's see a really full rotation of those shoulders - put everything into it!

Work hard on getting the ball to swing as **close** to the batter as possible

85

In-swing Bowling

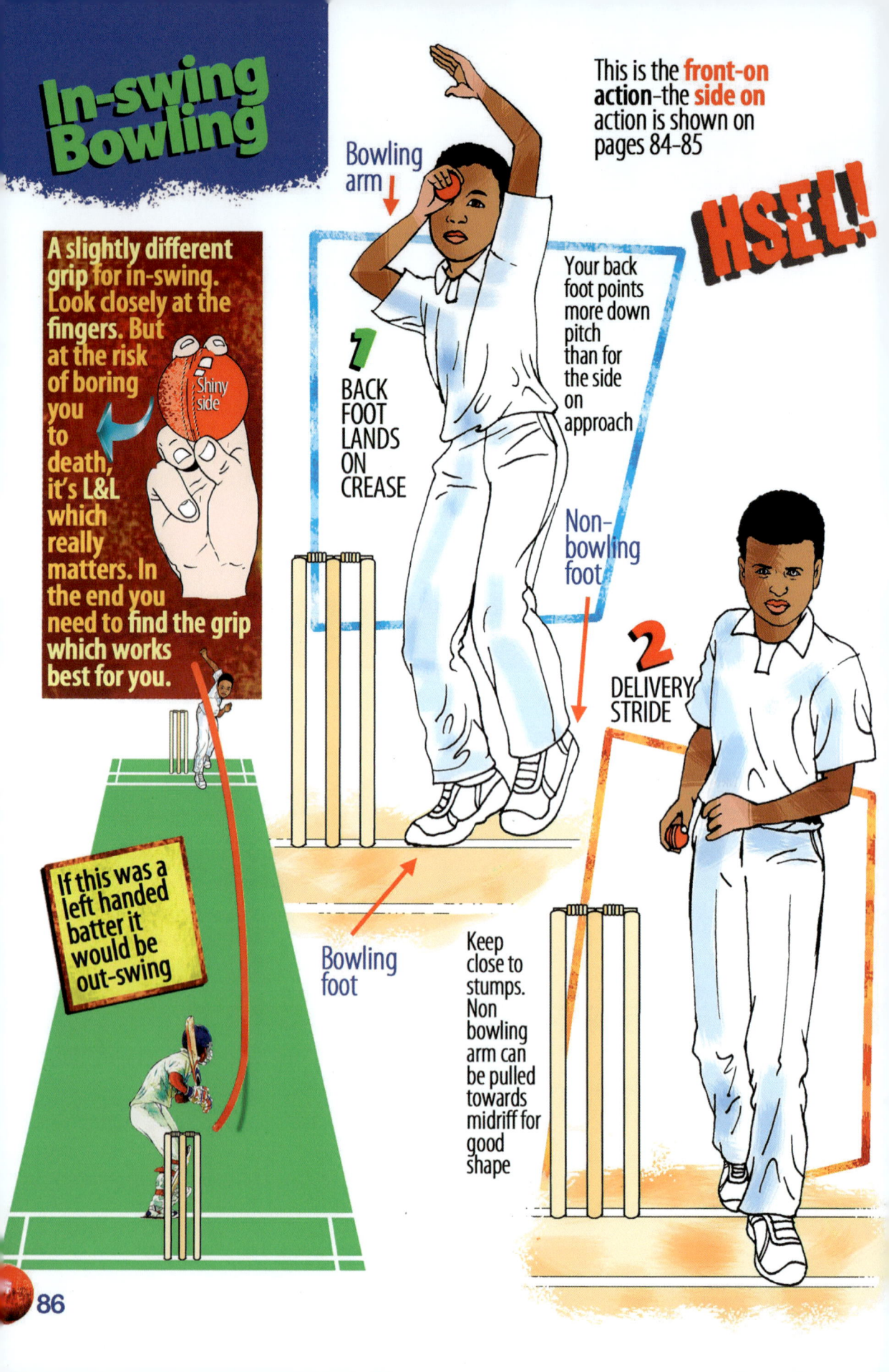

A slightly different grip for in-swing. Look closely at the fingers. But at the risk of boring you to death, it's L&L which really matters. In the end you need to find the grip which works best for you.

Shiny side

If this was a left handed batter it would be out-swing

This is the **front-on action** - the **side on** action is shown on pages 84-85

Bowling arm

HSEL!

1 BACK FOOT LANDS ON CREASE

Your back foot points more down pitch than for the side on approach

Non-bowling foot

2 DELIVERY STRIDE

Bowling foot

Keep close to stumps. Non bowling arm can be pulled towards midriff for good shape

86

SKILL SHEET

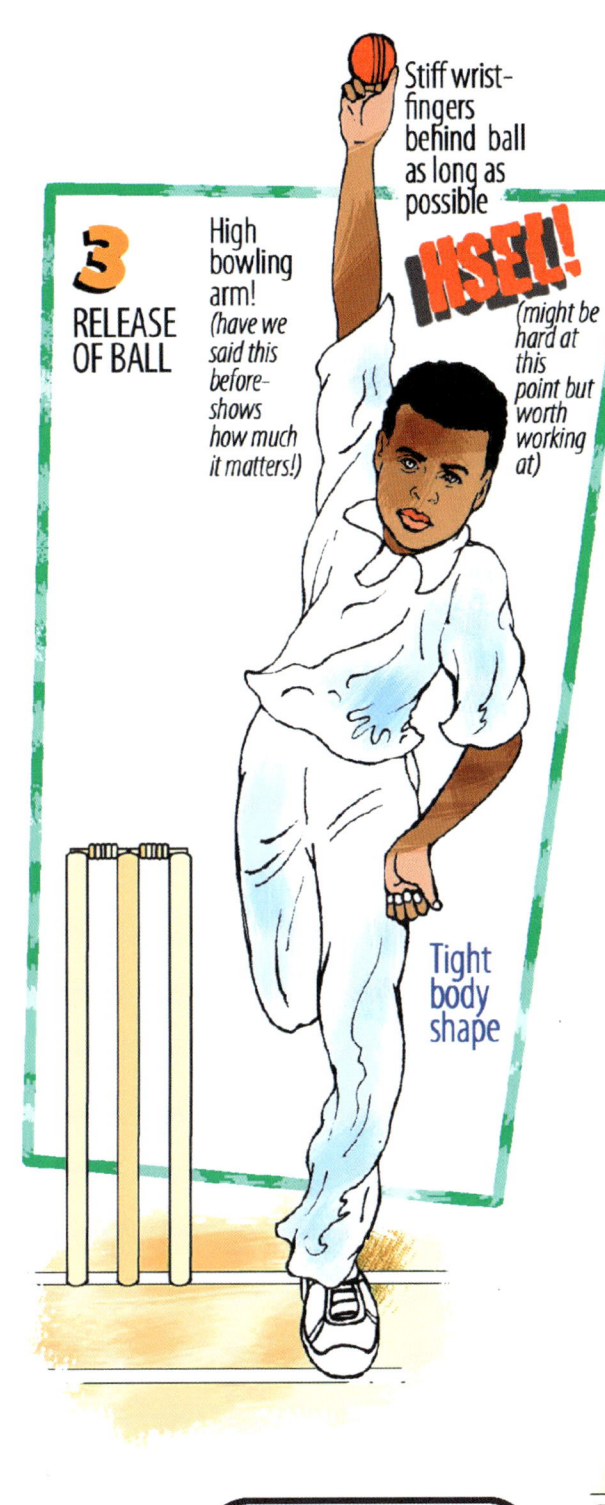

3 RELEASE OF BALL

Stiff wrist - fingers behind ball as long as possible

High bowling arm! (have we said this before - shows how much it matters!) (might be hard at this point but worth working at)

YSEL!

Tight body shape

The big danger with in-swing is it's so easy to miss your line and spray it down the leg side - so a tight off stump line is so vital if you're going to bother the batter - and you want to make the batter's life very unpleasant! Are we going to go on about practice again? YES! YES! YES!

4 FOLLOW THROUGH

Fling the non bowling arm high and back in the follow through

Powerful rotation of shoulders - back leg drives through

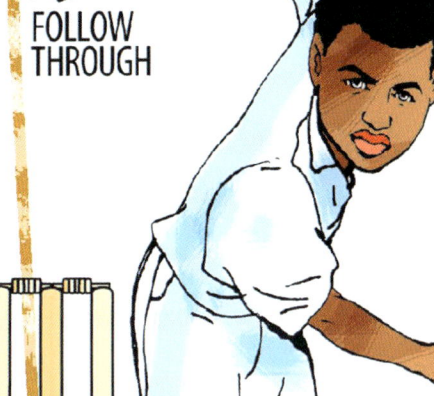

Your aim is to hit the stumps! Look for the gap between bat and pad as the batter plays forward to the good length ball.

87

ABOUT SPIN BOWLING

Good spinners are like snake charmers

The spin bowler wants to deceive and confuse the batter. The ball is tossed high so that the batter has to look up and lose balance and be unsure of what the ball is doing. If the ball is spun enough it can be tossed high and will drop quickly on reaching the batter.

YOU MIGHT GET HIT FOR SIX...

...but if a batter takes risks as long as you don't lose your nerve and keep your length and direction mistakes will come...

Which fielder was hoping to catch this?

...like the stumping...

...the catch in the deep...

...the catch off the edge.

Don't be afraid to give the ball lots of spin – the movement off the pitch is your best weapon

Deep point

89

Off-spin

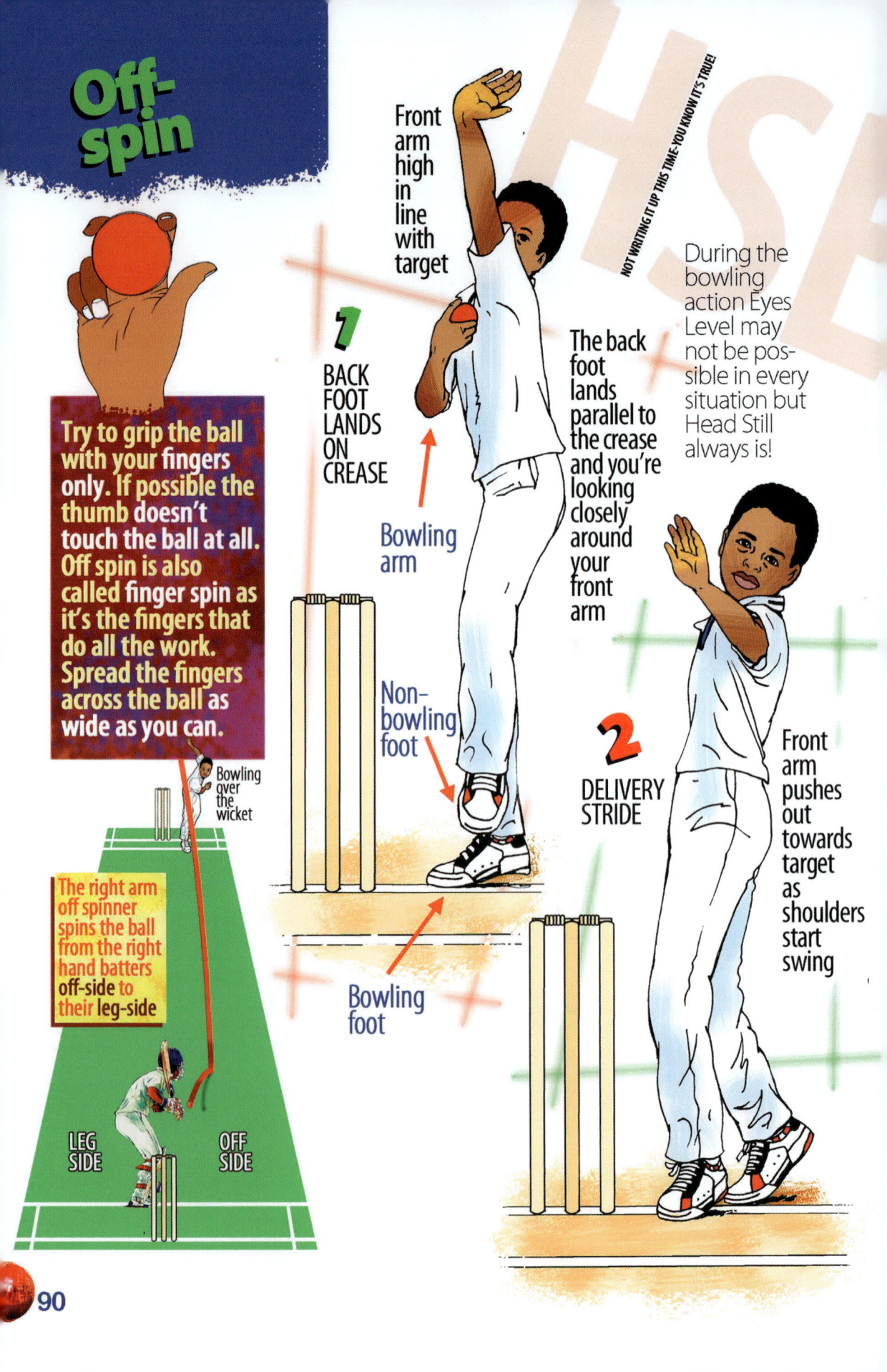

Try to grip the ball with your **fingers** only. If possible the **thumb** doesn't touch the ball at all. Off spin is also called finger spin as it's the fingers that do all the work. Spread the **fingers across the ball** as wide as you can.

The right arm off spinner spins the ball from the right hand batters **off-side** to their **leg-side**

Bowling over the wicket

LEG SIDE — OFF SIDE

1 BACK FOOT LANDS ON CREASE

Front arm high in line with target

Bowling arm

The back foot lands parallel to the crease and you're looking closely around your front arm

Non-bowling foot

Bowling foot

NOT WRITING IT UP THIS TIME-YOU KNOW IT'S TRUE!

During the bowling action Eyes Level may not be possible in every situation but Head Still always is!

2 DELIVERY STRIDE

Front arm pushes out towards target as shoulders start swing

90

SKILL SHEET

3 RELEASE OF BALL

Your bowling arm is below vertical

Before the ball is released your hand looks like a swan's head pointing left

Weight pushes through braced front leg

4 FOLLOW THROUGH

Full follow through- strong shoulder rotation to the left pocket

Hips rotate over front foot as back leg drives through

Lift left heel on delivery

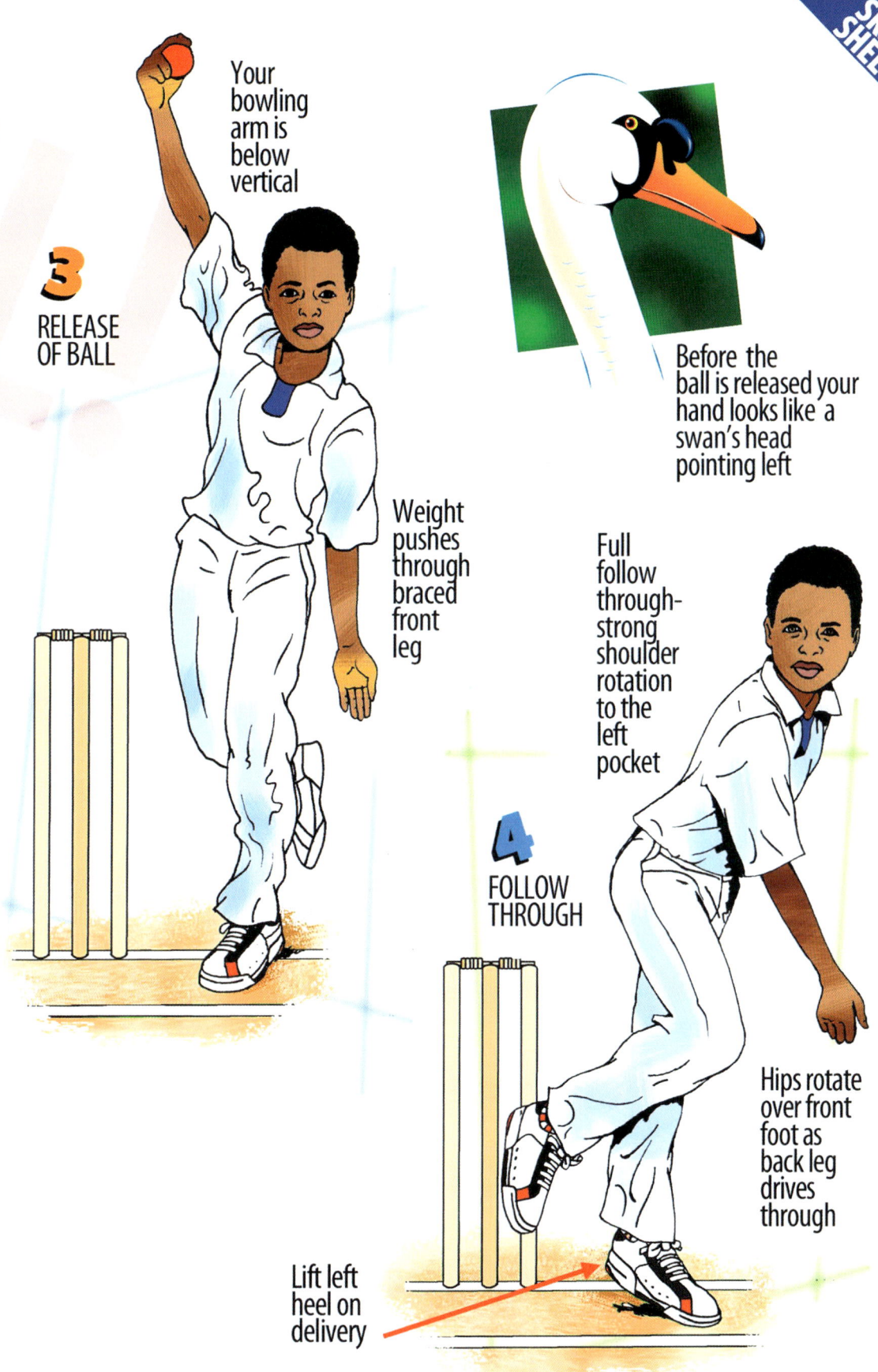

91

ABOUT OFF-SPIN

It's a hot day. The fast bowlers are tired, the pitch is dusty. The captain throws you the ball. You toss it up, spinning it hard. It bites off the pitch and moves across the surprised batter and she misses it and is LBW! **Maybe it's your day!**

The off spin bowler has the same two jobs as all bowlers- to take wickets and stop batters scoring runs. The ball is spun from left to right and the ball moves from left to right...

The action is exactly like turning a door knob.

...off spin bowlers will try to fool the batter into thinking they can be slogged everywhere. (If you bowl short that's exactly what will happen!)

To bowl a different flight, finish your run a bit **behind** the crease or **release the ball a bit earlier**. Both methods need a lot of practice. It's always wise to work on getting control of **length and line** first.

THE STAGES OF OFF-SPIN

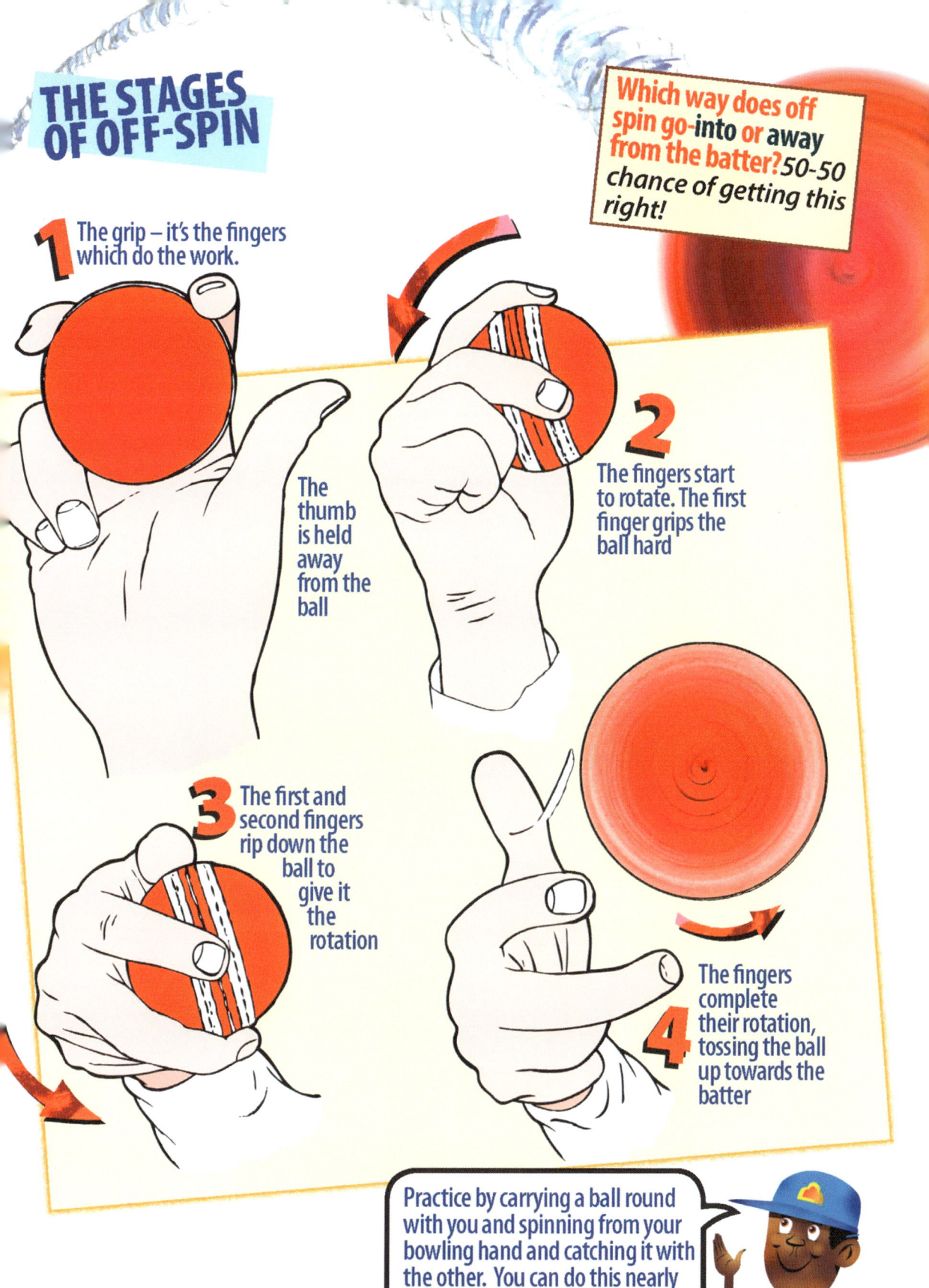

Which way does off spin go - into or away from the batter? 50-50 chance of getting this right!

1 The grip – it's the fingers which do the work.

The thumb is held away from the ball

2 The fingers start to rotate. The first finger grips the ball hard

3 The first and second fingers rip down the ball to give it the rotation

4 The fingers complete their rotation, tossing the ball up towards the batter

Practice by carrying a ball round with you and spinning from your bowling hand and catching it with the other. You can do this nearly anywhere.

Into

93

Leg spin

The ball is controlled by the **first three fingers** As for all bowling the ball is **held in the fingers**, not pushed into the palm of your hand. Work hard to get **a lot of spin**-you will be all over the place at first but it's the spin which makes you dangerous. Accuracy and control will come **(with hard work!)**

Non-bowling arm

Bowling arm

1 BACK FOOT LANDS ON CREASE

The back foot lands parallel to the crease and you're looking around your front arm

Non-bowling foot

Bowling foot

2 DELIVERY STRIDE

Front arm pushes out towards target as shoulders start swing

LEG SIDE   OFF SIDE

94

Wrist cocked

Your bowling arm is below vertical

3 RELEASE OF BALL

Before you let the ball go your hand looks like a swan's head pointing right

Weight pushes through braced front leg

4 FOLLOW THROUGH

Full follow through- strong shoulder rotation

Hips rotate over front foot as back leg drives through

SKILL SHEET

Make sure you really **rip** that spin- don't just lob it up-the ball needs to **bite** off the surface.

95

MORE ABOUT LEG SPIN

It is very difficult to bowl leg spin with **accuracy** and **control**. That's why there aren't many leg spinners about. But that's also why batters don't like them – they rarely have the chance to practice against them!

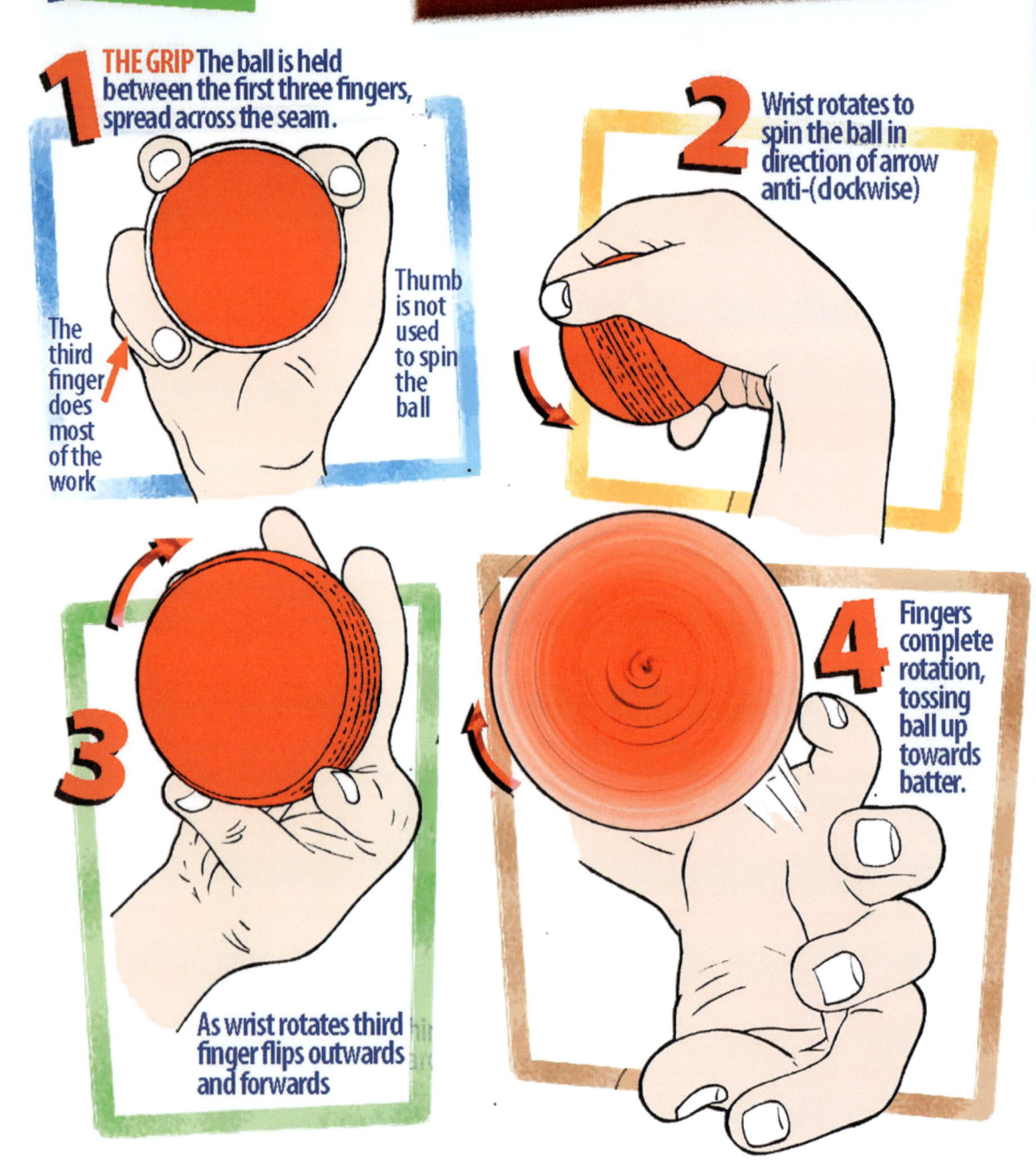

STAGES OF LEG SPIN

1. THE GRIP The ball is held between the first three fingers, spread across the seam.

The third finger does most of the work

Thumb is not used to spin the ball

2. Wrist rotates to spin the ball in direction of arrow anti-(clockwise)

3. As wrist rotates third finger flips outwards and forwards

4. Fingers complete rotation, tossing ball up towards batter.

ANSWERS: 1. Away from batter towards slips 2. In

96

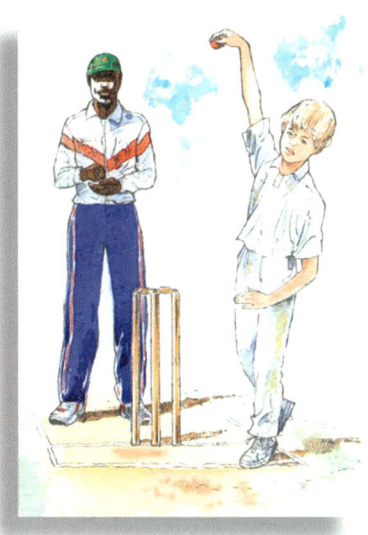

YOU ARE LOOKING FOR WICKETS...

Keep the ball **well up** to the batter-short balls are a gift from a spinner. As a leg spinner you will get hit from time to time- don't give up! **You are a rare and protected species!**

A leg spinner. Which way does it go? Should I come out and go out for it, or should I stay in my crease and see what happens?

There are many ways of spin bowling – the googly, the floater, the doosra, the arm ball - work hard and you will find your **own** way to spoil the batter's party!

Bowling is difficult – only by **constant practice** can you get the control you need – but when you get it right and run through a side there's no better feeling!

1 Which way does leg spin go?
2 Which way to a left hander?

The wrist gives the spin and movement off the pitch. That is why leg spin is also called **wrist spin.**

97

ABOUT WICKET KEEPING

Next time you go to see some cricket, spend some time watching the wicket keeper.

The keeper is never still. At first standing a long way back with the ball speeding into the gloves and sometimes having to dive to left or right.

Often running up to the stumps or sometimes removing a glove and chasing the ball into the outfield.

Then later in the innings moving up to the stumps as the spinners come on, looking for close catches or stumpings. And all the time geeing up the fielders.

Sometimes the captain will come up and ask the keeper's advice on field placings or how to get a batter out.

The keeper needs to be able to catch with either hand. It's a tough job, but exciting and always right in the action.

A good wicket keeper improves the whole side and puts pressure on the batters.

WICKET KEEPERS' EQUIPMENT

HELMET At under 15 a wicket keeper must wear a helmet standing up

GLOVES New gloves can be stiff. Work them in a bit with some catching practice before you wear them in a match. It's a good idea to use cotton inners.

BOX Essential for boys. Never keep without a box and have a proper support for it.

PADS If you are serious about wicket keeping it's best to get proper keeper's pads rather than use your batting pads. Keeper's pads are lighter and that bit more flexible which you will be glad of if you keep for long periods.

FOOTWEAR tough flexible trainers with good grip are essential but studs are not necessary for under 11's.

Look at the coaching sheet on the next page. What is the keeper doing right with his:

1 Eyes
2 Hands
3 Fingers
4 Body position

Try to answer the questions without looking back at the coaching sheet.

ANSWERS 1 Watching ball 2 Together 3 Pointing down 4 Crouched just outside off stump

Every team needs a good keeper. You'll never be out of a job with this skill!

Wicket keeping

STANDING UP
Always try to take the ball as close to the bat as possible

Wicketkeeping is an exciting job, and you need to be fit. You are always in the action and have to concentrate on every ball. You need to learn about how the ball will spin or swing, bounce or keep low and also have a good knowledge of field placings. You need to be able to cheer up your side and be full of energy and enthusiasm. I bet you can't wait to get started!

1 THE STANCE
You need to be comfortable, balanced and be able to move speedily in any direction. Crouch close to the ground on the balls of feet. Fingers lightly on ground between legs, pointing outwards. Left foot behind off and middle stumps. No part of wicketkeeper should be in front of stumps or a 'no ball' will be called.

2 THE LOW TAKE
Start from the stance. Keep head and body behind the ball. Rise with the bounce of the ball. Fingers pointing down and hands in front of body. Give with the ball as it comes into your gloves. Don't snatch out at the ball, wait for it to come to you.
Watch the ball into your hands. Take it underneath your eyes.

Outside foot moves across

THE HIGH TAKE
Rise with the ball and watch it into your hands. Give with your hands as you take the ball.

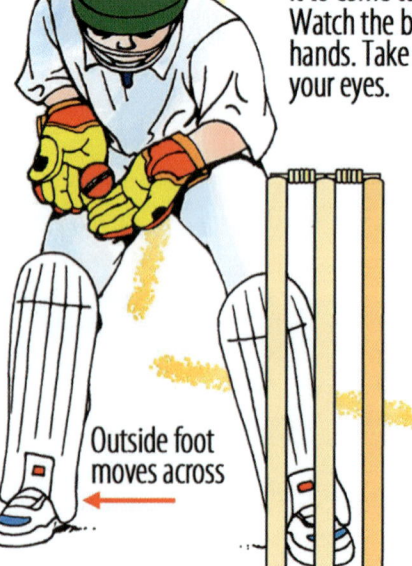

SKILL SHEET

HSEL – as always!

3 THE OFF SIDE TAKE
Move your outside foot and your body towards the line of the ball. Try to keep the inside leg fixed in position. You might have to get up on your toes to reach the ball.

4 THE LEG SIDE TAKE
Exactly as the Off side take except you move the inside leg.

5 STUMPING
Rise with the ball and watch it off the bat into your hands. Give with your hands as you take the ball. Feet remain in position. Knees flex as body moves towards stumps. Always try to use both hands.

Outside foot turns slightly inwards

> Keep your hands **low** before taking the ball - it's easier moving your hands **up** than moving them **down**

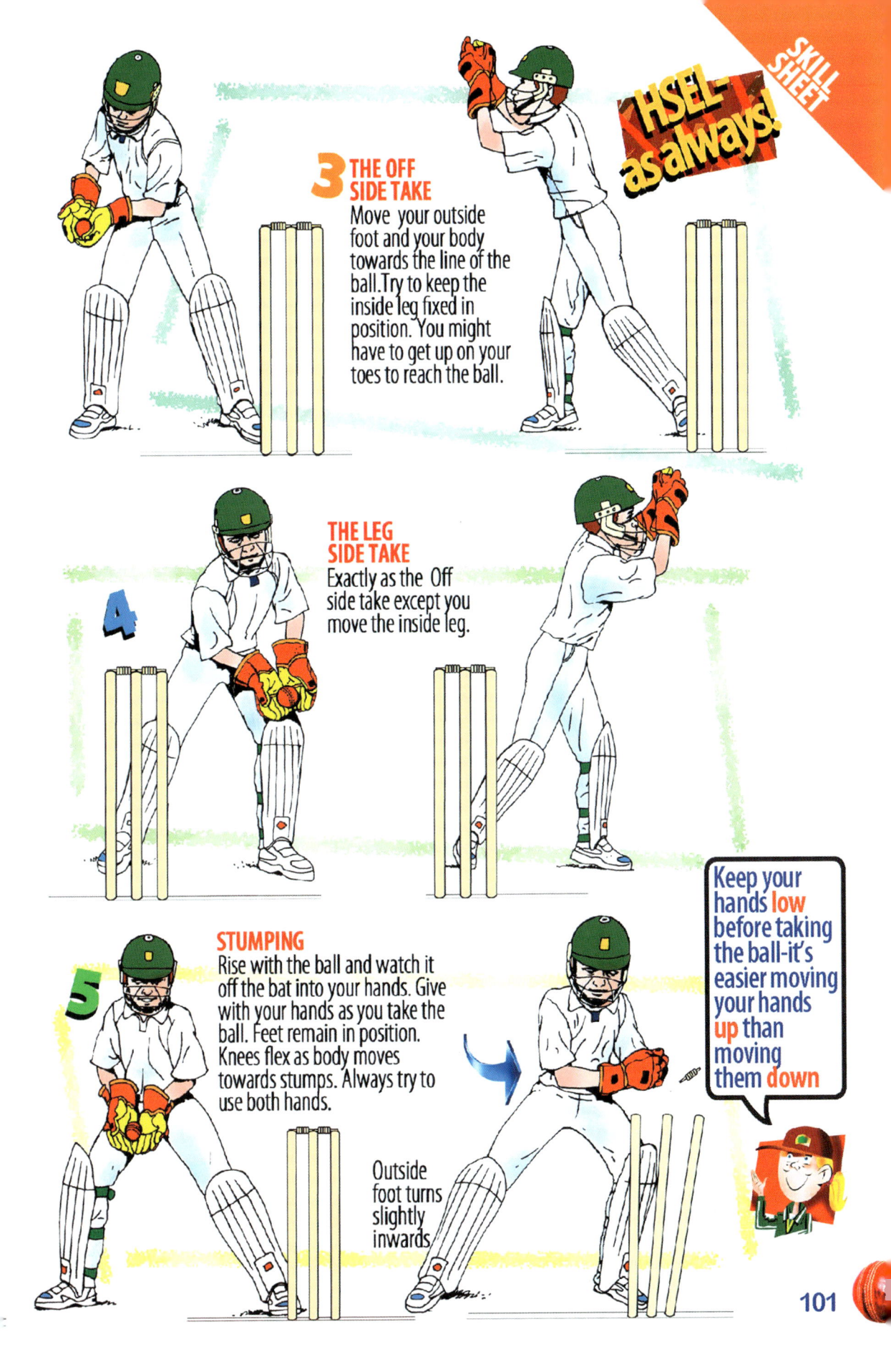

101

Wicket keeping

When the ball goes out in the field you should **run up to the stumps and face the line of the ball,** ready for the return–but sometimes you may need to chase the ball, remove the glove from your throwing hand and try for a run out–as wicketkeeper you have to be ready for **anything!**

STANDING BACK

1

STANCE
Crouched, not so low as standing up, slightly to batters off side to give a clear view of the bowler and far enough back to take the ball when it begins to drop.

STRAIGHT TAKE
Move quickly across to catch the ball with your head and body right behind it. Hands ride with the ball.

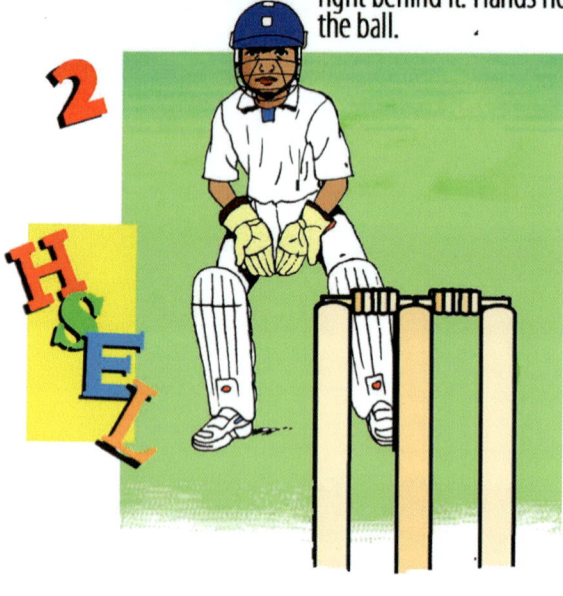

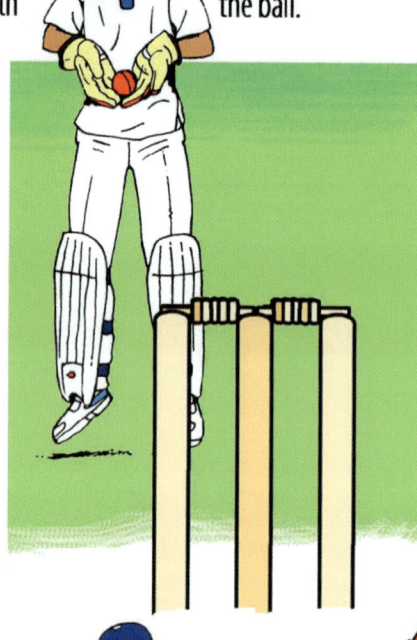

Rise with the bounce of the ball.

2

THE OFF SIDE TAKE
Your feet and body move to the off side to get the head in line with the path of the ball using a side step. Weight on balls of feet. Rise with the bounce of the ball. Hands give.

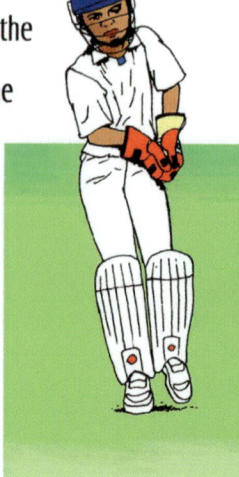

3

4 THE LEG SIDE TAKE

Exactly as the Off side take except you move the to the leg side.

If the ball bounces high always move your head to one side as you take it.

DIVING
If you have to dive...

Dive flat and take the ball as late as possible. Roll on landing to avoid injury and jarring and to make sure you don't drop the ball.

Always watch the ball from the bowler's hand into your gloves. Keep low, head still, eyes level as bowler delivers the ball. Rise with the bounce of the ball. Don't push your hands out to meet the ball, let it come to you and give with your hands as the ball enters your gloves. Even with a wild throw try to take the ball with your gloves and not your pads.

Don't get fanatical about stumpings. Watch the ball, wait for it, take the ball correctly and stumpings will follow naturally. Watch the ball, not the batter.

Always try to take the returns from the field in the gloves

UMPIRE'S SIGNALS

These signals are worth getting to know. You might get a chance to umpire someday. It's a great job and you get the best ever view of the cricket.

FOUR

SIX

OUT

BYE

LEG BYE

If the ball hits the batter or their pads and they take a run this is called a **leg-bye**

WIDE

SHORT RUN

If your bat does not go over the crease at the end of your run the umpire will signal to the scorers and you lose a run

NO-BALL

DEAD BALL

No need for tears! When the ball is in play it is 'live'. If something happens such as a fielder moving or talking after the bowler has started the run up the umpire may call 'dead ball' and the ball has to be re-bowled

OTHER SIGNALS
(In professional cricket)

POWER PLAY **FREE HIT**

Without umpires cricket wouldn't work. They run the match.

105

WAYS OF GETTING OUT

There are 10 ways of getting out

These are the ones that you will mostly see and they are all very obvious:

Caught
Bowled
LBW
(Leg Before Wicket)
See diagram opposite
Run out
Stumped
Hit wicket

THESE ARE RARE:

Handled the ball
(You can kick the ball away to stop it rolling on to the stumps but you are not allowed to use your hands)
Hit the ball twice
(You are not allowed to deliberately hit the ball again after you've already hit it)
Obstructing the field
(Deliberately hindering the fielders)
Timed out
(Only happens in senior cricket)

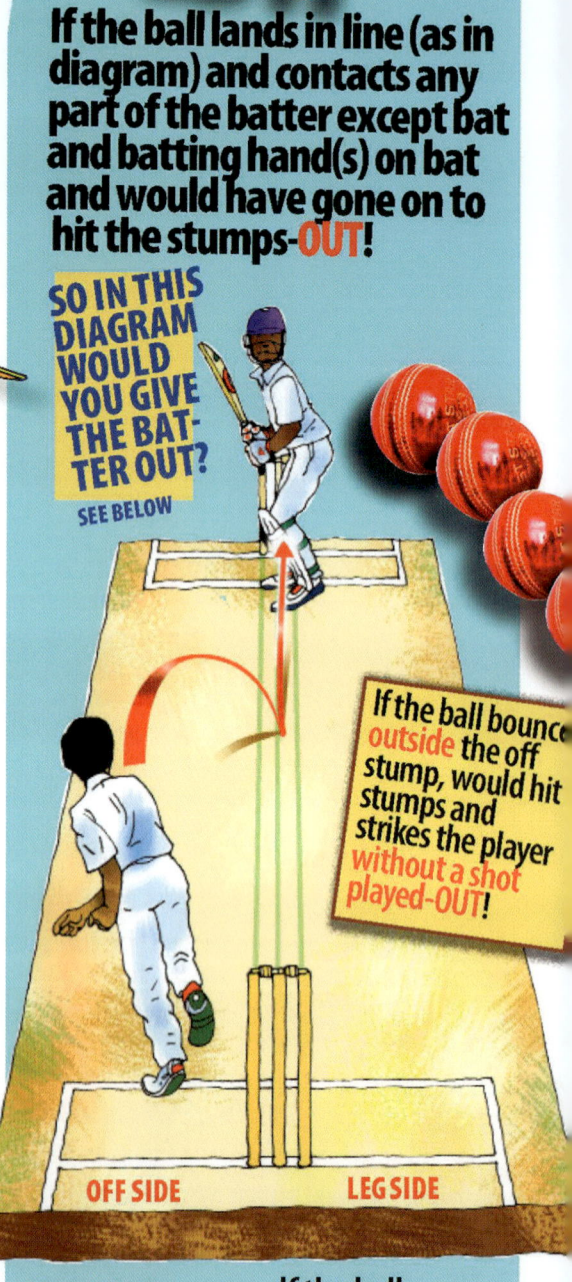

LBW

If the ball lands in line (as in diagram) and contacts any part of the batter except bat and batting hand(s) on bat and would have gone on to hit the stumps–OUT!

SO IN THIS DIAGRAM WOULD YOU GIVE THE BATTER OUT?
SEE BELOW

If the ball bounces *outside* the off stump, would hit stumps and strikes the player *without a shot played*–OUT!

OFF SIDE — LEG SIDE

If the ball **touches the bat before hitting the player** the batter **cannot be out LBW**.

If the ball bounces on the **leg side** the batter **cannot be out LBW** even if it would have hit the stumps.

Yes

TYPES OF NO-BALL

The first three are the ones you mostly need to know about:

Overstepping front crease
(Often called the popping crease) Whole of foot must be beyond line-if the foot or part of the foot is **behind** the line, even in the air it is not a no-ball

Ball bounces more than twice

Ball reaches batter above waist height without bouncing

The next four are the umpire's business but worth knowing:

Throwing -bowling with bent arm (lots of beginners do this-the coach will sort it out)

Bowlers foot lands outside or on return crease

Some part of wicket keeper is in front of the stumps

More than two fielders behind square on leg side

Bowler attempts to run out striker or non striker before delivery of ball

107

CAPTAIN & SPIRITS

You have all heard about the captain of a ship. His or her job is to look after the crew and make certain everything works properly. Every cricket team also has a captain who is the boss and in charge of the team. Here are some of the things a captain will do:

- Meet the captain of the other team and spin a coin (call 'heads or tails'). This is called winning or losing the toss and the winning captain can choose whether their team bats or bowls first

- Agree the batting order. There are nomally 11 players and everyone wants to bat first but someone has to bat last- number 11

- When the team is bowling the captain must decide who bowls and in what order. The captain must also decide- usually after chatting with the bowler- the fielding positions of every player. The wicket keeper is easy- always behind the stumps but where the other players' field will depend on where the batters are hitting the ball.

"Can you go to square leg please-that's where the ball's going, more chance of a catch!"

Be enthusiastic and encourage everyone in the team

"Good effort, hard luck!"

Another important job of the captain is to make certain that the team are always **sporting** and follow the laws. This is called the 'spirit of the game'.

ALWAYS

- **Play fair**
- Be polite to your team mates and opponents
- Clap the other side when new batters come in
- Shake hands with your opponents at the end of the game and thank the people who have helped, umpires and scorers and anyone who has provided drinks and biscuits

NEVER

- Laugh or cheer if an opponent makes a mistake
- Sulk, kick the ground or throw your bat if you are out.
- Say nasty things to opponents to put them off. This is called 'Sledging'
- Grumble at your team mates if they make a mistake
- Say bad things on social network sites

ALWAYS

Support your captain even if you don't agree with every decision.

HOW TO SCORE

Buy a scorebook (or drop a birthday hint) and try it out while watching cricket-good fun and good practice.

The scorebook is in 2 main sections. **Batting** and **Bowling** and 2 smaller sections, **Fall of Wickets**, **Extras** and **Totals**, and 2 boxes for ticking off the score as you go (**Run Count** and **Over Count**)

SYMBOLS

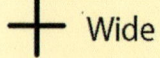

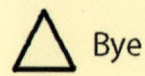

- ⊙ No-ball
- + Wide
- △ Bye
- ▽ Leg bye
- W Wicket

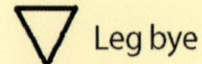

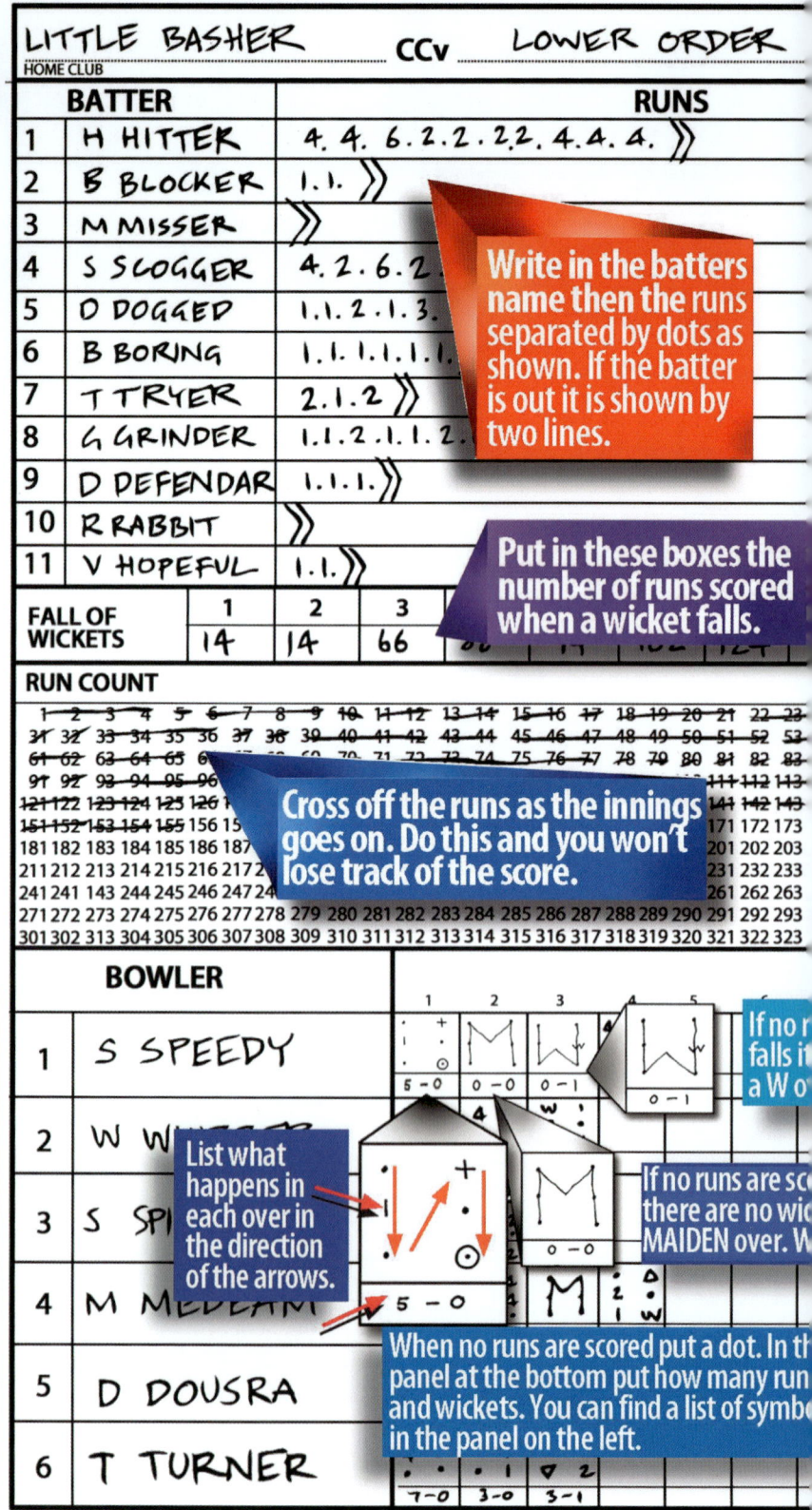

HOME CLUB: LITTLE BASHER   **CCv**   LOWER ORDER

	BATTER	RUNS
1	H HITTER	4. 4. 6. 2. 2. 2. 2. 4. 4. 4. 》
2	B BLOCKER	1. 1. 》
3	M MISSER	》
4	S SLOGGER	4. 2. 6. 2.
5	O DOGGED	1. 1. 2. 1. 3.
6	B BORING	1. 1. 1. 1. 1. 1.
7	T TRYER	2. 1. 2 》
8	G GRINDER	1. 1. 2. 1. 1. 2.
9	D DEFENDAR	1. 1. 1. 》
10	R RABBIT	》
11	V HOPEFUL	1. 1. 》

Write in the batters name then the runs separated by dots as shown. If the batter is out it is shown by two lines.

FALL OF WICKETS	1	2	3
	14	14	66

Put in these boxes the number of runs scored when a wicket falls.

RUN COUNT

1 2 3 4 5 6 7 8 9 10 11 12 13 14 15 16 17 18 19 20 21 22 23
31 32 33 34 35 36 37 38 39 40 41 42 43 44 45 46 47 48 49 50 51 52 53
61 62 63 64 65 66 67 68 69 70 71 72 73 74 75 76 77 78 79 80 81 82 83
91 92 93 94 95 96 ... 111 112 113
121 122 123 124 125 126 ... 141 142 143
151 152 153 154 155 156 15... 171 172 173
181 182 183 184 185 186 187 ... 201 202 203
211 212 213 214 215 216 217 ... 231 232 233
241 241 143 244 245 246 247 24... 261 262 263
271 272 273 274 275 276 277 278 279 280 281 282 283 284 285 286 287 288 289 290 291 292 293
301 302 313 304 305 306 307 308 309 310 311 312 313 314 315 316 317 318 319 320 321 322 323

Cross off the runs as the innings goes on. Do this and you won't lose track of the score.

	BOWLER	1	2	3	4	5	6
1	S SPEEDY						
2	W W...						
3	S SP...						
4	M M...						
5	D DOUSRA						
6	T TURNER						

List what happens in each over in the direction of the arrows.

If no runs are scored there are no wickets MAIDEN over. W...

If no r... falls it... a W o...

When no runs are scored put a dot. In the panel at the bottom put how many runs and wickets. You can find a list of symbols in the panel on the left.

110

of: **LOWER ORDER** DATE —/—/— PLAYED AT **L ORDER RD**

HOW OUT	BOWLER	RUNS
c CACHA	S SPINNER	34
lbw	W WHIZZER	2
bowled	S SPEEDY	0
c HANDY		44
NOT		17
c and b		6
bowled	W WHIZZER	5
run	out	9
c CACHA	M MEDEAM	3
c GLOVER	T TURNER	0
bowled	S SPEEDY	2

Put in these boxes how the batter got out and their score.

WIDES	2.2.2.2.2.2.2	15
NO BALLS	2.2.2	6
BYES	1.3.1.1.	9
LEG BYES	1.1.1.	3

Put the extras in these boxes then add all the totals up at the end of the innings.

TOTAL BATTERS RUNS 122
EXTRAS 33
TOTAL EXTRAS 33

FOR ...10... WICKETS ...20... OVERS **TOTAL SCORE** 155

MAIDENS	RUNS	WKTS	AVG
2	18	1	18.00
–	23	2	11.50
–	29	2	14.50
		1	26.00
–	33	2	16.50
–	14	1	14.00

This section is filled in after the match is over. Don't worry about it until you get more used to scoring.

OVER COUNT

OVERS	RUNS	OVERS	RUNS
1	14	27	
2	36	28	
3	62	29	
4	76	30	
5	92	31	
6	93		
7	93		
8	94		
9	102		
10	107		
11	111		
12	111		
13	115		
14	129		
15	137		
16	141		
17	143		
18	145		
19	151	45	
20	155	46	
21		47	
22		48	
23		49	
24		50	
25		51	
26		52	

Put the number of runs scored in every over in these boxes, adding up as you go. Another way to avoid losing count of the score.

UMPIRES
D DEADEYE
P SPOTTER

SCORERS
S STICKLE
B BOOKM

PLAYER of the MATCH
B BELTER
(LITTLE BASHER)

Nice if you can fill in this box but not essential

On the next page is a scoresheet for you to copy ▶

111

HOME CLUB .... **CCv** .... innings of: ___

	BATTER	RUNS
1		
2		
3		
4		
5		
6		
7		
8		
9		
10		
11		

FALL OF WICKETS	1	2	3	4	5	6	7	8	9

RUN COUNT

```
  1   2   3   4   5   6   7   8   9  10  11  12  13  14  15  16  17  18  19  20  21  22  23  24  25  26  27
 31  32  33  34  35  36  37  38  39  40  41  42  43  44  45  46  47  48  49  50  51  52  53  54  55  56  57
 61  62  63  64  65  66  67  68  69  70  71  72  73  74  75  76  77  78  79  80  81  82  83  84  85  86  87
 91  92  93  94  95  96  97  98  99 100 101 102 103 104 105 106 107 108 109 110 111 112 113 114 115 116 117
121 122 123 124 125 126 127 128 129 130 131 132 133 134 135 136 137 138 139 140 141 142 143 144 145 146 147
151 152 153 154 155 156 157 158 159 160 161 162 163 164 165 166 167 168 169 170 171 172 173 174 175 176 177
181 182 183 184 185 186 187 188 189 190 191 192 193 194 195 196 197 198 199 200 201 202 203 204 205 206 207
211 212 213 214 215 216 217 218 219 220 221 222 223 224 225 226 227 228 229 230 231 232 233 234 235 236 237
241 241 143 244 245 246 247 248 249 250 251 252 253 254 255 256 257 258 259 260 261 262 263 264 265 266 267
271 272 273 274 275 276 277 278 279 280 281 282 283 284 285 286 287 288 289 290 291 292 293 294 295 296 297
301 302 313 304 305 306 307 308 309 310 311 312 313 314 315 316 317 318 319 320 321 322 323 324 325 326 327
```

	BOWLER	1	2	3	4	5	6	OVERS 7	8	9
1										
2										
3										
4										
5										
6										

DATE .... PLAYED AT ....

	HOW OUT	BOWLER	RUNS

WIDES

NO BALLS

BYES

LEG BYES

TOTAL EXTRAS

FOR............. WICKETS.............OVERS

				MAIDENS	RUNS	WKTS	AVG
11	12	13	14				

OVER COUNT

OVERS	RUNS	OVERS	RUNS
1		27	
2		28	
3		29	
4		30	
5		31	
6		32	
7		33	
8		34	
9		35	
10		36	
11		37	
12		38	
13		39	
14		40	
15		41	
16		42	
17		43	
18		44	
19		45	
20		46	
21		47	
22		48	
23		49	
24		50	
25		51	
26		52	

TOTAL BATTERS RUNS

EXTRAS

TOTAL SCORE

UMPIRES

SCORERS

PLAYER of the MATCH

JOIN A CRICKET CLUB

It's great playing cricket in the park with friends, or on the beach or even in the street if it's safe.

But if you want to go a bit further, you can't beat joining a cricket club. If you look around you're likely to find a club close to you and they are often looking for new players.

Here you will get coaching and matches against other teams. You will make friends and find others who are mad about cricket, too. And that can't be bad.

It's not the same everywhere, but usually you will fill in a registration form and pay a subscription for the year. Then will come the first coaching evening when you will meet the other players of your age, some of whom will be new, just like you.

You will find the coaches will try to make you feel at home and help you to enjoy your training.

At some clubs the first training evening of the summer is a fun time with continuous cricket or an all session game.

The coaches will explain what they want you to do.

For younger players some clubs organize soft ball cricket tournaments after school.
You may also get to practice in the nets – always with an adult present and proper protection (see batting sheets).
Before you know it you will be playing matches against opposition of your own age with umpires, scorers, the whole works. There are cup competitions and league competitions. Of course if you improve you may get a chance to play for your county, and eventually your country! Almost every international cricketer came up through the club system
There are lots of good things that happen in a cricket club.
You get advice, training, use of the club's facilities, and a chance to watch good quality cricket at your own ground.

Usually clubs have a festival in the summer where there is lots of junior cricket. Many families organize their holidays round the club's cricket week! **Warn your parents now!**
At the end of the season some clubs have an end of season celebration of some kind where awards are handed out.
And during the winter, in England you get indoor cricket leagues and some clubs will have pre-season coaching – so you could be playing cricket all the year round!
You might get to go on tour with your club – some clubs even tour abroad.

100 UP QUIZ
CAN YOU REACH YOUR CENTURY?
(without looking at the answers on the next page!)

1 What fielders sound as if they're about to fall over?
2 What does it mean when the umpire puts a finger up?
3 What does LBW stand for?
4 What is the stitched bit around the ball called?
5 What is the cut area between the stumps called?
6 When you are in the deep or ring field what should you do when the bowler is running up?
7 A leg spinner is also called a w x x x x spinner
8 Can a batter be LBW if the ball bounces outside leg stump?
9 What is the batter who is not hitting the ball called?
10 When does the wicketkeeper stand up?
11 What can you do to the ball to help it swing?
12 What does the umpire's signal patting leg mean?
13 How many balls in an over?
14 How do you score a four?
15 What does HSEL mean?
16 Which fielder is good at cleaning up?
17 How do you hold the ball when throwing? a x x x x t x x s x x x
18 Name one way a batter can be OUT
19 What are the 3 upright wooden sticks called?
20 What is the edge of the field called?
21 What is meant by LINE?
22 What is a MAIDEN over?
23 In the stance where should your back foot be?
24 What are the names of the stumps?
25 What can happen when taking a run if you don't have your bat on the ground at the end of your run?
26 Should you use your thumb for Off-spin?
27 How do you score a six?
28 Why do you hold the ball across the seam when throwing?
29 For catching fingers P x x x x D x x x
30 What is meant by 'attack the ball'?
31 When would you use Long Barrier?
32 What is a good length?
33 What is meant when the umpire has one hand in the air?
34 What is a WICKET MAIDEN?
35 Is it a no-ball if your foot lands on the front crease?
36 Where does the umpire not at the bowlers end stand?
37 Where should the wicketkeeper stand when the fielders are chasing the ball?
38 Umpire puts both arms in air. What does it mean?
39 Another name for Off-spin
A Hand spin B Arm spin C Finger spin D Slip spin E Turn F Wobble spin
40 What is it called if a ball bowled bounces lots of times?
41 Are you out if you are caught and it's a no-ball?
42 What is the batter who is about to hit the ball called?
43 Are you out LBW if the ball brushes the bat before it hits the pad?
44 How many umpires are there?
45 In bowling what is meant by swing?
46 Which way does the ball move in Leg spin? to the Oxx xxxx
47 What is the player in charge of the team called?
48 Which foot should you land on when you bowl? ONN GIBWLON
49 What is the player behind the stumps at the batters end called?
50 In the forward defensive stroke which hand does all the work?
51 What birds head does a spinners hand look like?
52 Is the batter out stumped if the back foot is on the line?

116

53 When does a keeper stand back?
54 What does this symbol mean? +
55 What is the line in front of the stumps called?
56 It is a no-ball if the ball bounces more than ECWIT?
57 Where should a standing up keeper crouch?
58 What does this symbol mean? ⊙
59 The umpire waves one hand horizontally-what does it mean?
60 If you're right handed which is your non-bowling foot?
61 When would you use one hand pick up and throw?
62 How high should your elbow be when throwing?
63 What do you do with your head when taking a skim catch?
64 What are the two bits of wood on top of the stumps called?
65 Which knee is on the ground for Long Barrier? N x x x x x x x x x x
66 Umpire touches shoulder -why?
67 Are you allowed to question umpires decisions?
68 When can you stump a batter?
69 What stump should you aim at when bowling?
70 What does LENGTH mean?
71 What is the non strikers call area?
72 What is a BAD length?
73 Where does the ball go from a Square Cut: A Point B Square Leg C Fine Leg C Cow Corner D Gully
74 Are you out if you hit the stumps with your bat when the ball is bowled?
75 Umpire extends both arms-why?
76 Are you out if you are bowled and it's a no-ball?
77 Another name for leg spin
A Thumb Spin B Palm spin C Knuckle spin D Wrist spin E Head spin
78 For fast bowling you hold the seam RHGPUTI
79 To what ball do you play the Back Foot Drive? A Good Length B Short on Stumps C Outside Leg Stump D Bouncer C Outside off stump
80 What happens if you step over the crease when you bowl?
81 Where does the ball go in a Pull Shot? A Third Man B 1st Slip C Into the Pond D Square Leg E Long Off
82 What if the umpire crosses hands in front of body?
83 What is the Strikers call area?
84 Where should your front foot land when you bowl?
85 What is a BAD line?
86 When do you play a Back Foot Drive? THROS NO SPUMST
87 Is a ball which reaches the batter above waist height without bouncing OK?
88 Why is your bowling or throwing hand always opposite to the non-bowling or non-throwing foot?
89 What does it mean when umpire holds out one arm?
90 Which hand does the work in the Square Cut?
91 If you're left handed which is your non-bowling foot?
92 What fielding move is named after a bird?
93 What kind of ball is right for a Pull Shot? S x x x x O x x x x x x L x x S x x x x
94 What part of field would mid wicket be? A Deep B Middle C Ring D Leg E Off F Close G Middle Earth
95 What ball needs a Forward Defensive? DGOO LNHETG
96 If you run off the pitch and hit a very very wide ball is it still a wide?
97 If the ball bounces on the leg side and would hit the stumps can the batter be LBW?
98 When running between wickets what should you call if you're not sure if there is a run?
99 How many ways are there to be out?
100 Can a batter score runs off a no-ball?

ANSWERS

Did you make the big 100?
(without looking back through the book?)

1 Slips 2 Out
3 Leg before wicket 4 Seam 5 Pitch
6 Walk in 7 Wrist spinner 8 No
9 Non striker 10 To a slow bowler (spinner is correct) 11 Polish one side
12 Leg bye 13 Six 14 Batter hits the ball across the boundary either along the ground or with at least one bounce
15 Head still eyes level 16 Sweeper
17 Across the seam
18 Caught, bowled, LBW, stumped, run out, hit wicket, hit ball twice, handled ball, obstructing field, timed out.
19 Stumps 20 Boundary
21 Direction of ball from bowler's hand (If you said direction of ball OK)
22 An over in which the batter scores no runs and there are no wides or no-balls
23 Behind the front crease
24 Off, middle, leg 25 You can be run out 26 No 27 Batter hits the ball over the boundary in air without it bouncing
28 For accuracy 29 Point down
30 When fielding run to the ball don't stand and wait for it to come to you
31 In deep field 32 Ball bouncing close up to batter when bowled
33 Bye 34 No runs off bat, no no-balls or wides and a wicket. 35 No
36 Square leg
37 At the stumps 38 Six

39 Finger spin 40 No - ball
41 No 42 Striker 43 No 44 Two
45 Movement of ball in the air
46 Off side 47 Captain
48 NON BOWLING
49 Wicketkeeper 50 Top 51 Swan
52 Yes 53 To fast bowling
54 Wide 55 Crease 56 Yes (Twice)
57 Outside Off stump
58 No-ball 59 Four runs 60 Left
61 Close to stumps looking for a run out 62 Above or level with shoulder
63 Move it to one side 64 Bails
65 Non throwing 66 Short run- batter's bat was not over crease at the end of the run 67 No 68 If foot is not BEHIND crease after ball has passed batter 69 Off 70 Point where ball bounces when bowled 71 Behind the striker
72 Short 73 A Point 74 Yes
75 Wide 76 No
77 D Wrist spin 78 UPRIGHT
79 B Short on stumps 80 Umpire calls no-ball 81 Square leg
82 Dead ball 83 In front of the bat
84 On the front Crease
85 Wide 86 SHORT ON STUMPS
87 No, it's a no-ball
88 For balance
89 No-ball 90 Bottom
91 Right 92 Crow hop
93 Short outside leg stump
94 C Ring 95 GOOD LENGTH 96 No
97 No 98 Wait 99 10 100 Yes

119

STATISTICS

Stats are fun and keeping a record helps you to see how you've improved - as a player and as a team.

BEST BATTING/FIELDING

DATE	RUNS	OPPOSITION	4's	6's	CATCHES

BEST BOWLING

DATE	OVERS	MDNS	RUNS	WKTS	OPP

BEST TEAM SCORES

DATE	SCORE	WKTS	OPP	BEST BATTER	BEST BOWLER	RESULT

PUZZLE 1

Some questions to refresh your memory - answers p 126

1 What shot?
2 Where does the ball go?

3 What shot is played to this ball?

4 How about this ball?

5 For what type of bowling would you use this grip?

6 Can you name this fielder? (Right handed batter)

Wicket keeper

122

7 What shot?
8 Which fielder would be stopping this?

11 What type of swing?

9 What fielder?
10 What area of the field?

12 Which is the non-bowling foot?
13 Which type of spin bowler?

123

PUZZLE 2

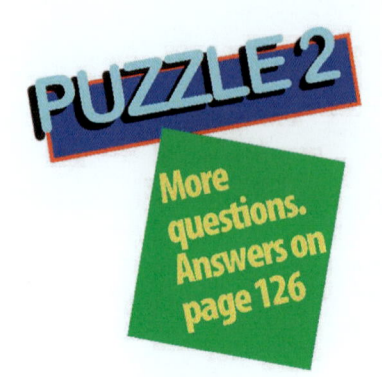

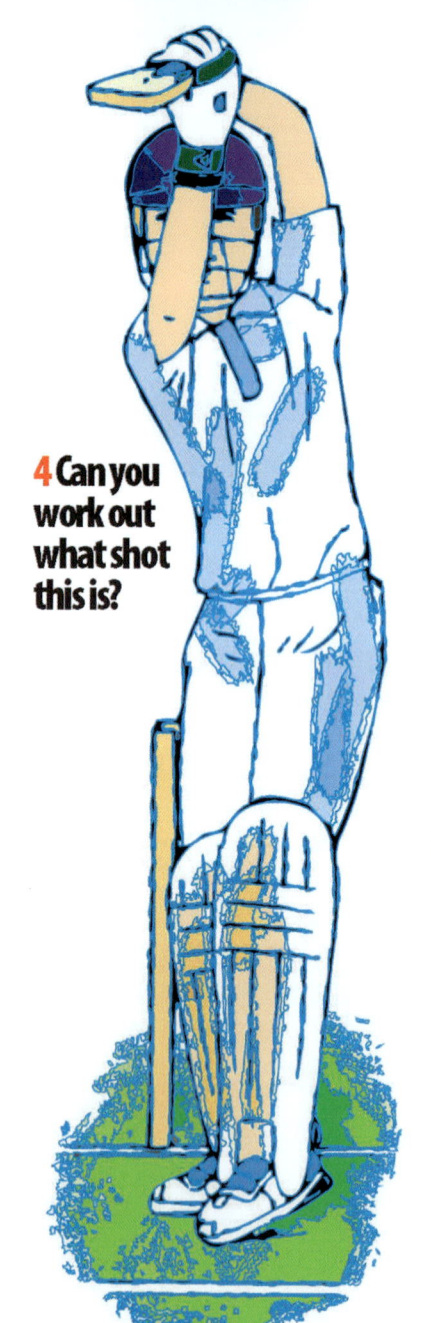

More questions. Answers on page 126

Wicket keeper

1 What is this fielding position? (Right handed batter)

2 What shot?
3 Where should the ball go?

4 Can you work out what shot this is?

5 Can you name these fielders?

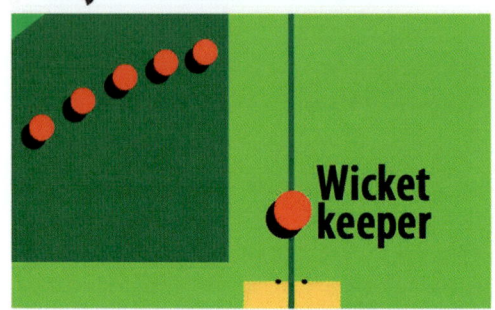

Wicket keeper

6 Foot movement for what shot?

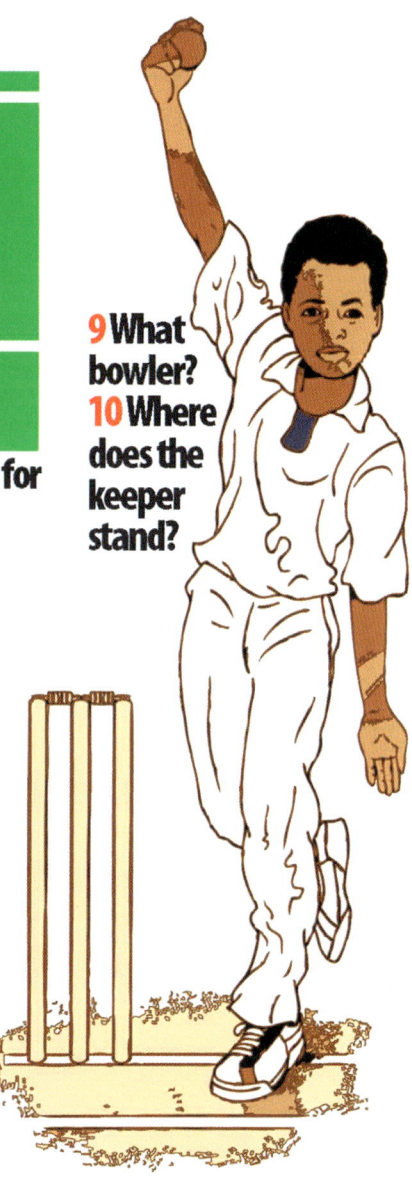

7 What does this signal mean?

8 Grip for what type of bowling?

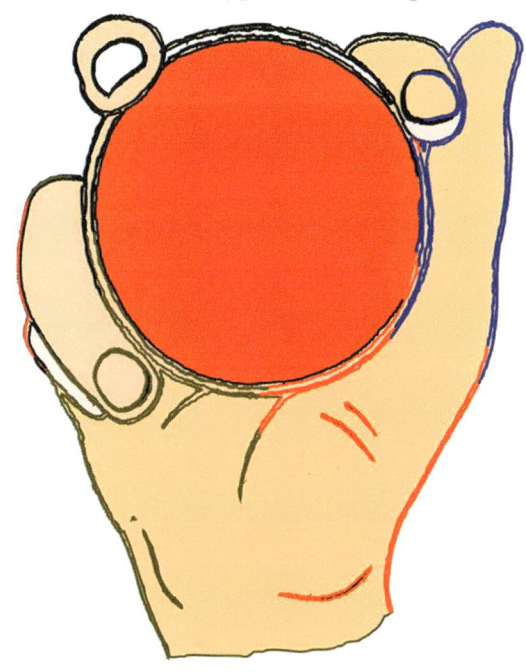

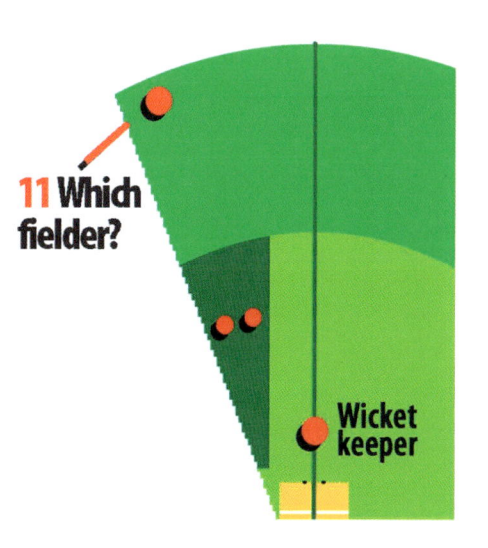

9 What bowler?

10 Where does the keeper stand?

11 Which fielder?

Wicket keeper

125

ANSWERS

PAGES 122-123

1 Forward defensive 2 Into the ground in front of batter 3 Back defensive 4 Pull 5 Seam 6 Mid on 7 Pull 8 Square leg 9 Long barrier 10 Deep 11 Out 12 Left 13 Leg spinner

PAGES 124-125

1 Square leg 2 Square cut 3 Point 4 Back foot drive 5 Slips 6 Pull 7 Short run 8 Leg spin 9 Off spinner 10 Up to the stumps 11 Third man

127

ENJOY YOUR CRICKET!

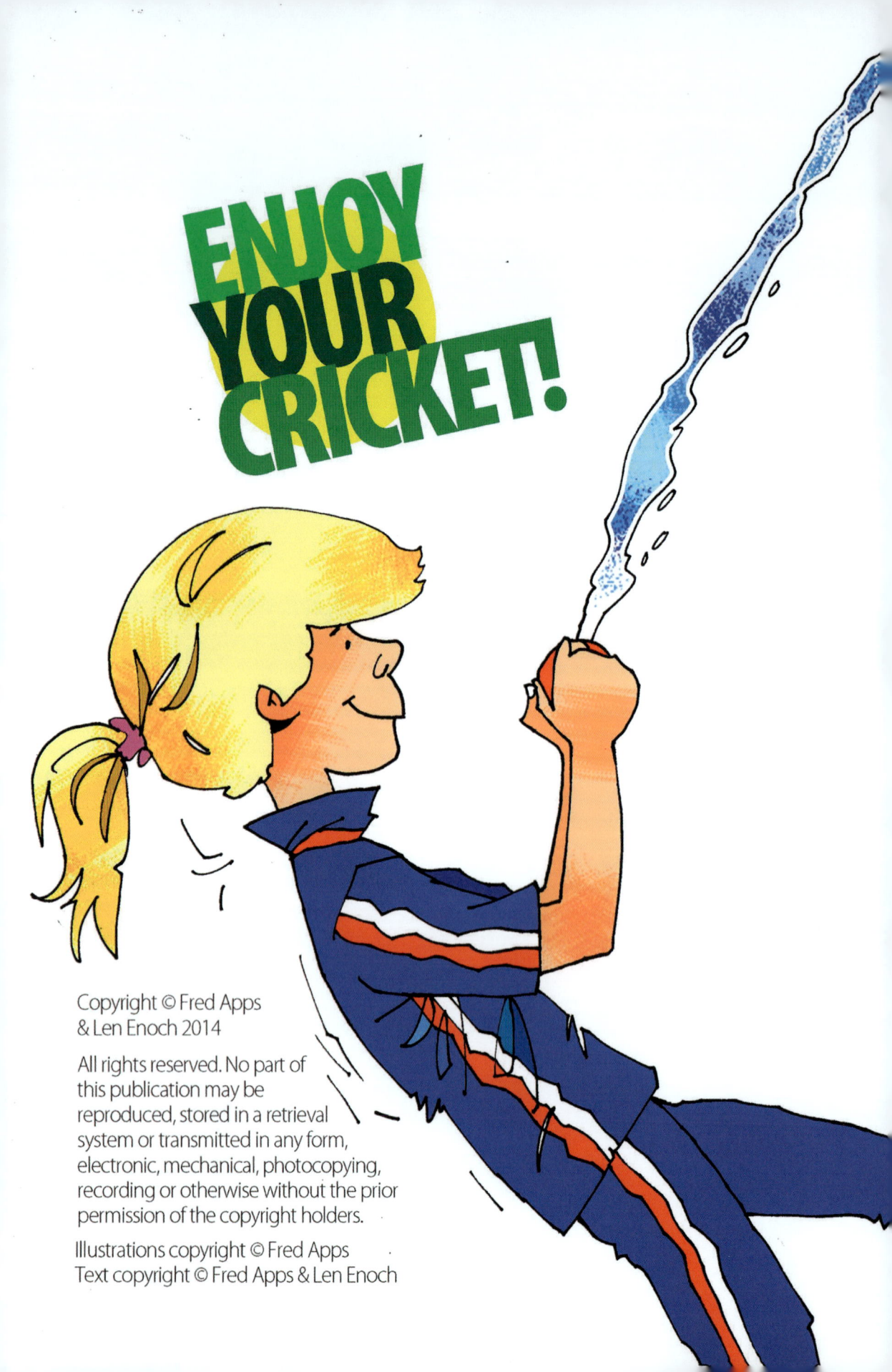

Copyright © Fred Apps
& Len Enoch 2014

All rights reserved. No part of this publication may be reproduced, stored in a retrieval system or transmitted in any form, electronic, mechanical, photocopying, recording or otherwise without the prior permission of the copyright holders.

Illustrations copyright © Fred Apps
Text copyright © Fred Apps & Len Enoch

Printed in Great Britain
by Amazon